Benin:

Malaria Operational Plan FY 2014

TABLE OF CONTENTS

ABBREVIATIONS and ACRONYMS

ACT	Artemisinin-based combination therapy
AfDB	African Development Bank
AL	Artemether-lumefantrine
ANC	Antenatal care
ARM3	Accelerating the Reduction of Malaria Morbidity and Mortality
BCC	Behavior change communication
CAME	*Centrale d'Achat des Médicaments Essentiels* (Central Medical Stores)
CCM	Country Coordinating Mechanism
CDC	Centers for Disease Control and Prevention
CHW	Community health worker
CREC	*Centre de Recherche Entomologique de Cotonou* (Center for Entomological Research – Cotonou)
CRS	Catholic Relief Services
CY	Calendar year
DHS	Demographic and Health Survey
EUV	End-use verification
FY	Fiscal year
GHI	Global Health Initiative
Global Fund	The Global Fund to Fight AIDS, Tuberculosis, and Malaria
GOB	Government of Benin
HMIS	*Système National d'Information et de Gestion Sanitaire* (Health Management Information System)
iCCM	Integrated community case management
IMCI	Integrated management of childhood illnesses
IPTp	Intermittent preventive treatment of malaria in pregnancy
IRS	Indoor residual spraying
IRSP	*Institut Régional de Santé Publique* (Regional Institute of Public Health)
ITN	Insecticide-treated net
LIAT	Logistics Indicator Assessment Tool
LLIN	Long-lasting insecticide-treated net
LMIS	Logistics management information system
MCDI	Medical Care Development International
M&E	Monitoring and evaluation
MICS	Multiple Indicator Cluster Survey
MIP	Malaria in Pregnancy
MIS	Malaria Indicator Survey
MOH	Ministry of Health
MOP	Malaria Operational Plan
NGO	Non-governmental organization
NMCP	*Programme National de Lutte Contre le Paludisme* (National Malaria Control Program)
O-P	Organophosphate
OR	Operations Research
PC	Peace Corps

PCV	Peace Corps Volunteer
PITA	*Plan Intégré du Travail Annuel (Annual Integrated Work Plan)*
PMI	President's Malaria Initiative
PSD	*Plan Stratégique de Développement*
RAMU	*Régime d'Assurance Maladie Universelle* (National Health Insurance System)
RBM	Roll Back Malaria
RDT	Rapid diagnostic test
RMIS	Routine Malaria Information System
SP	Sulfadoxine-pyrimethamine
UNICEF	United Nations Children's Fund
USAID	United States Agency for International Development
USG	United States Government
WARN	West Africa RBM Network
WHO	World Health Organization
WHOPES	World Health Organization Pesticide Evaluation Scheme

I.   EXECUTIVE SUMMARY

Malaria prevention and control are major foreign assistance objectives of the U.S. Government (USG). In May 2009, President Barack Obama announced the Global Health Initiative (GHI) to reduce the burden of disease and promote healthy communities and families around the world. The President's Malaria Initiative (PMI) is a core component of the GHI, along with HIV/AIDS, tuberculosis, maternal and child health, family planning and reproductive health, nutrition, and neglected tropical diseases.

PMI was launched in June 2005 as a 5-year, $1.2 billion initiative to rapidly scale up malaria prevention and treatment interventions and reduce malaria-related mortality by 50% in 15 high-burden countries in sub-Saharan Africa. With passage of the 2008 Lantos-Hyde Act, funding for PMI was extended and, as part of the GHI, the goal of PMI was adjusted to reduce malaria-related mortality by 70% in the original 15 countries by the end of 2015. Programming of PMI activities follows the core principles of GHI: encouraging country ownership and investing in country-led plans and health systems; increasing impact and efficiency through strategic coordination and programmatic integration; strengthening and leveraging key partnerships, multilateral organizations, and private contributions; implementing a woman- and girl-centered approach; improving monitoring and evaluation; and promoting research and innovation.

In December 2006, Benin was selected to receive funding during the third year of PMI. In Benin, malaria is endemic nationwide and is a major cause of morbidity and mortality. It is reported to account for 40% of outpatient consultations and 25% of all hospital admissions. With 37% of the population living below the poverty line and a per capita annual income of only $750, malaria places an enormous economic strain on Benin's development. According to the World Bank, households in Benin spend approximately one quarter of their annual income on the prevention and treatment of malaria. The most recent Demographic and Health Survey (DHS), conducted from December 2011 to March 2012, showed significant improvements in several key indicators compared to the last DHS of 2006. These indicators included net ownership and usage, and uptake of intermittent preventive threatement of pregnant women (IPTp), to name a few.

The Global Fund to fight AIDS, Tuberculosis, and Malaria (Global Fund) awarded two malaria grants to Benin that were operational through 2012. Catholic Relief Services (CRS) was approved for a transitional funding mechanism (TFM) for $7,050,000 to implement malaria case management in 14 health zones. Africare was approved for a Phase 2 proposal for $37.5 million to procure 85% of LLINs to distribute during the nationwide campaign scheduled for 2014. Also, PMI will cover the remaining needs and the distribution costs. The World Health Organization (WHO), the United Nations

Children's Fund (UNICEF), and other national and international partners continue to support scaling-up of malaria prevention and control measures in Benin.

This FY 2014 Malaria Operational Plan (MOP) is based on progress and results to date, as well as input received from the National Malaria Control Program (NMCP) and its partners during a PMI planning visit in March 2013. The activities that PMI is proposing complement the contributions of other partners and directly support the NMCP's strategic plan. To achieve PMI's goals and targets in Benin, the following major activities will be supported with FY 2014 funding at a proposed $16.1 million level:

Insecticide-treated bed-nets (ITNs): The NMCP strategy (2011-2015) supports free distribution of long-lasting insecticide-treated nets (LLINs) through: antenatal care (ANC) and immunization services provided at health facilities; distribution of highly-subsidized LLINs through community-based channels such as women's groups and cooperatives; free distribution of LLINs through mass campaigns, and the sale of LLINs in the commercial sector. The NMCP has recently proposed the addition of a pilot school-based distribution strategy in three departments targeting school children from 5 to 11 years of age, who will not only bring home a bed net, but also learn and translate into local languages the appropriate messages for the use of those nets. This will be piloted as an option to maintain bed net coverage after a mass distribution campaign. In the meantime, PMI will work with NMCP and partners to update ITN policy, to develop the methods, and to identify appropriate indicators that will reflect meaningful outcome measures associated with this strategy. During the past year, PMI procured 510,000 LLINs, of which 385,000 were made available for routine distribution, 100,000 were to be sold through the commercial sector, and 25,000 were targeted for community distribution using locally developed strategies to fill gaps in coverage, handled by the Peace Corps. As PMI continues to support the government, it seeks to improve delivery of nets by strengthening the logistics management system and by promoting their use through behavior change activities. Moreover, PMI has funded LLIN tracking studies to determine their longevity and durability, with findings soon to be published. These activities have contributed to the observed increase in ITN ownership from 25% in 2006 to 80% in 2012, according to the DHS. With FY 2013 and 2014 funding, PMI will procure a total of 800,000 LLINs for routine and national campaign distribution and will pilot LLIN distribution through primary schools.

Indoor residual spraying (IRS): The NMCP's strategy aims to scale up IRS so that 20 of 77 communes are covered by 2015. To date, only PMI is supporting IRS in Benin, currently focusing on nine communes in the northern department of Atacora, where only one spray round per year is needed due to climatic conditions that limit vector breeding and malaria transmission. Based on this strategy, PMI sprayed 210,380 houses in 2012, protecting over 652,000 people. Also, PMI continues to monitor vector resistance to respond to concerns over the appropriate choice of insecticide and the additional costs to maintain protection of the target population. With FY 2014 funding, PMI will continue support for IRS in the department of Atacora, targeting approximately 210,000 houses, while maintaining surveillance efforts to ensure effectiveness of the intervention.

Malaria in pregnancy (MIP): Benin's 2011-2015 national strategy supports a multi-pronged approach to MIP. The policy supports free distribution of sulfadoxine-pyrimethamine (SP) and LLINs to pregnant women presenting to their first ANC clinic visit. Results from the 2012 DHS showed that 86% of women made at least one ANC visit during their last pregnancy. Although an increase from <1% in the 2006 DHS, uptake of SP for IPTp still remained low, at 23% in 2012, despite the high ANC attendance rate by pregnant women. The 2011 ITN 'universal coverage campaign' may have contributed to an increase in the proportion of pregnant women who slept under an ITN; from 20% in 2006 to 71% according to the 2012 DHS. During the past 12 months, PMI provided approximately 680,000 LLINs and over one million doses of SP for use in ANC facilities. Using FY 2014 funds, PMI will procure LLINs (cited above) and approximately one million doses of SP for routine delivery and treatment at public and private health facilities. Also, PMI will work closely with the Clinical Case Management Technical Working Group to facilitate the incorporation of the updated WHO MIP guidelines into Benin's national strategy. Additional PMI support will include a rapid qualitative assessment, strengthening of logistics management, training and supervision of health workers in IPTp, and supporting behavior change and communication (BCC) activities to educate pregnant women and communities on the risks of MIP.

Case management – Diagnosis: PMI continues to support a comprehensive diagnostics strengthening program that involves the training of clinicians and laboratory technicians, the implementation of a quality control and quality assurance system, strengthening supervision to ensure that health workers follow clinical practice guidelines, and provision of diagnostic commodities such as rapid diagnostic tests (RDTs). During the past year, supervision to maintain and improve the quality of microscopy was conducted in 118 health facilities (90% were public facilities and 10% were private). Supervision is performed in the 118 sites with laboratory facilities and emphasizes observing the administration of RDTs during routine clinical consultations. Supervision was semestral for 72 of the facilities and quarterly for 46 facilities. Quality scores were 86% for slide preparation and 88% for slide reading. As well, PMI will have purchased 1.5 million RDTs to cover needs for 2014 and basic materials for the reparation and maintenance of the existing microscopes. In addition, 118 advanced-user guides for the laboratory diagnosis of malaria will be developed and disseminated in the health facilities. Despite the progress made in malaria diagnosis, 32% of patients under five with a negative RDT or microscopy result were treated with an artemisinin-based combination therapy (ACT) according to a health facility survey completed in April 2012. With FY 2014 funding, PMI will continue to work on improving the prescription to diagnostic ratio. This support will include the procurement of approximately 1.7 million RDTs (over half of the projected nationwide gap), 15 microscopes and reagents, as well as training and supervision of staff to better ensure that prescription of ACTs is based on a positive diagnostic result.

Case management – Treatment: In 2011, the NMCP updated its malaria case management guidelines to recommend universal diagnostic testing for malaria and free malaria treatment for all children under five and pregnant women (launched in October of that year). The main challenge for the free treatment policy is the process of reimbursing facilities, which has been slow, and possibly has led to overuse of certain presentations of ACTs, namely the lower weight bands, which are the only forms being reimbursed under the current guidelines. Working collaboratively with the NMCP, PMI will help resolve outstanding issues with regard to this policy. In addition, PMI has trained 772 health workers and continues to support training on the treatment protocol for uncomplicated malaria to service providers in the public and private sectors and continues to support supervision of uncomplicated malaria treatment at the outpatient level. During the past year, PMI procured 1.5 million ACTs and provided support for community case management of malaria. With FY 2014 funding, PMI will continue to support training and supervision of both public and private health care providers, including community health workers involved in community case management. Moreover, PMI will procure 1.5 million ACTs and support subsidization of the free treatment of uncomplicated malaria.

Case management – Pharmaceutical management: In order to support the NMCP strategy to strengthen the supply and distribution of malaria commodities, PMI has led the reform of several key components of the system, including the Central Medical Stores, *Centrale d'Achat des Médicaments Essentiels* (CAME), and the logistics management information system (LMIS). PMI support has included training of personnel, assistance for supervision, software and hardware for management of information, and technical assistance to help address new or outstanding issues. Although a great deal of support has been provided by multiple partners over several years, the supply chain system has many problems. However, PMI has identified two key issues that are currently being resolved: parallel commodity management systems developed for different donors and duplicative and uncoordinated commodity reporting systems. These weaknesses were causing continued stockouts in certain facilities and overstocks in others. With FY 2014 funding, PMI will continue the efforts implemented over the last few years to construct a more sustainable logistics and supply chain management system by implementing a set of targeted interventions which will focus on capacity building for the pharmaceutical and supply chain management systems. In collaboration with other stakeholders, PMI will work to strengthen malaria commodity supply chain management down to the facility level, strengthen the LMIS, and monitor the storage and distribution of malaria commodities. Additionally, PMI will support ACT quality control testing in-country.

Monitoring and evaluation (M&E): PMI has contributed to strengthening Benin's M&E systems, and the number of health facilities reporting timely data to the health management information system (HMIS) has significantly increased. During the last 12 months, PMI and NMCP staff worked closely on M&E issues and PMI resident advisors were active participants in the Benin M&E Technical Working Group. In 2012, there was a break in data reported from the sentinel surveillance sites; however activities have resumed and sites are currently collecting and submitting data. Surveillance data from the non-contract period was systematically collected from hospital registers and patient files, and complete supervision with quality control resumed in January 2013. A full assessment of the surveillance sites will be carried out in Benin during the next 12 months by the PMI M&E team who will provide recommendations on the continued support of the present surveillance system.

Additionally, PMI provided ongoing technical and financial assistance to the Routine Malaria Information System (RMIS) to conduct a quality audit and evaluation, provide supervision, and help build capacity through training in database management and analysis. To assess case management, availability of antimalarial drugs and diagnostic tests, PMI will support an end-use verification (EUV) survey to be implemented in the next 12 months. With FY 2014 funding, PMI will continue to support the health management information system (HMIS), sentinel surveillance, EUV surveys, an impact evaluation of national malaria control efforts, and a Malaria Indicator Survey (MIS).

Behavior change communication (BCC): The NMCP is planning to develop and implement a new integrated communication plan that will include strategies for advocacy, BCC, and social mobilization. As part of the process to develop this new plan, PMI supported a literature review to identify barriers to the use of IPTp and LLINs. The findings are being used as the basis for this new strategy and include, for example, increasing community engagement and upgrading BCC skills of health workers. Strong PMI support also led to the revitalization of the National Malaria Communications Working Group, which is responsible for reviewing the technical content of all BCC messages pertaining to malaria and will play a key role in developing an updated integrated communication plan. Regarding implementation of the BCC strategy, PMI supported a multi-pronged approach to reach the maximum number of beneficiaries using mass media, banners, messaging through community health workers, interpersonal communication in health centers, community events, the involvement of opinion leaders, and social marketing. With FY 2014 funding, PMI will support the continued rollout of the new integrated communication plan. PMI technical assistance will include providing reference documents; developing BCC strategies; facilitating partner meetings to discuss the development of the strategy; raising community and household awareness on the use of LLINs, recognizing signs of malaria, increasing care-seeking behavior, improving IPTp coverage; and supporting community mobilization for IRS. PMI-supported BCC activities will be implemented at both the national and community levels.

Health systems strengthening/capacity building: In the last three years, the NMCP and PMI have focused on three major challenges of the NMCP: (1) the lack of adequate human resource capacity - both in the number of staff and their skill set - to plan, manage, and coordinate a comprehensive malaria program; (2) the collection, management, and use of health information for M&E and surveillance purposes; and (3) the management of the health commodities supply chain, which is especially weak at the periphery, resulting in stockouts, and expired drugs and RDTs. To support the NMCP in addressing these challenges, PMI invested in the training of several key NMCP staff; supported the development of Technical Working Group (TWG) teams; supported the NMCP in conducting an evaluation of the existing HMIS; and supported the NMCP and CAME by reviewing current plans, training staff in areas of weakness, and assisting in the development of better tracking tools. The results of these actions have helped the NMCP better identify current gaps and allowed them to propose recommendations to address the gaps. With FY 2014 funding, PMI will continue to provide support for the staff training plan that was developed by the NMCP. The focus will include M&E, and will include training in database management, and support for the technical working group. Also, PMI will provide support for equipment and attendance at conferences and workshops related to logistics management.

II.   STRATEGY

A. INTRODUCTION

The President's Malaria Initiative (PMI) is a core component of the Global Health Initiative (GHI), along with HIV/AIDS, and tuberculosis. PMI was launched in June 2005 as a 5-year, $1.2 billion initiative to rapidly scale up malaria prevention and treatment interventions and reduce malaria-related mortality by 50% in 15 high-burden countries in sub-Saharan Africa. With passage of the 2008 Lantos-Hyde Act, funding for PMI was extended and, as part of the GHI, the goal of PMI was adjusted to reduce malaria-related mortality by 70% in the original 15 countries by the end of 2015. This will be achieved by reaching 85% coverage of the most vulnerable groups — children under five years of age and pregnant women with proven preventive and therapeutic interventions, including artemisinin-based combination therapies (ACTs), insecticide-treated nets (ITNs), intermittent preventive treatment of pregnant women (IPTp), and indoor residual spraying (IRS). The overall GHI Benin Country Strategy aims to achieve the GHI Objective of "improved health status of Beninese families" by focusing on four program areas: malaria prevention and control, maternal and child health, and reproductive health/family planning.

In December 2006, Benin was selected to receive funding during the third year of PMI. Since 2008, PMI has supported institutional capacity building, quality improvement in malaria prevention and care service delivery. In early FY 2012, most PMI activities were grouped under one malaria bilateral program, named Accelerating the Reduction of Malaria Morbidity and Mortality (ARM3), which continues to provide technical assistance to the National Malaria Control Program (NMCP) in areas of case management, supply chain management, behavior change communication (BCC), and monitoring and evaluation (M&E). Certain elements of the PMI program, such as IRS and commodities procurement, remain centrally managed to ensure that global standards are met.

This FY 2014 Malaria Operational Plan (MOP) presents a detailed plan for Benin, based on the NMCP's five-year strategy. It was developed in consultation with the NMCP, with participation of Benin PMI stakeholders and international partners involved with malaria prevention and control in the country. The activities that PMI is proposing build on investments made by PMI and other partners to improve and expand malaria-related services, including the Global Fund to Fight AIDS, Tuberculosis, and Malaria (Global Fund) grants. This document reviews the current status of malaria control policies and interventions in Benin, describes progress to date, identifies challenges and unmet needs of the targets to be achieved by the NMCP and PMI, and describes planned activities with FY 2014 funding.

B. MALARIA SITUATION IN BENIN

Epidemiology
According to 2011 health statistics from Benin's Ministry of Health (MOH), malaria is the leading cause of morbidity and mortality among children under five and among pregnant women. Roll Back Malaria (RBM) estimated that in 2004 there were about three million cases of malaria illnesses (all ages); and the World Health Organization (WHO)-convened Child Health Epidemiology Reference Group estimated that the number of malaria deaths in children 1–59 months old was about 10,000 in the year 2000 and about 9,000 in the year 2010. The 2012 Demographic and Health Survey (DHS) report states that malaria is responsible for 26% of hospitalizations overall and 44% of hospitalizations among children under five years of age. Data from Benin's Health Managagement Information System (HMIS) also suggest a high prevalence of anemia, which is likely caused by malaria. The Benin 2006 DHS found that among children 6–59 months old,

78% had anemia (25% mild, 46% moderate and 8% severe). Preliminary results of the 2012 DHS found that anemia prevalence in this age group decreased to 58% (26% mild, 29% moderate and 3% severe). Additional results from the 2012 DHS measured parasitemia prevalence in children under five at 28%.

Entomology/transmission (populations at risk of malaria)

Malaria transmission is stable but influenced by several factors such as vector species, geography, climate, and hydrography. The primary malaria vector in Benin is *Anopheles gambiae s.s.*, however, secondary vectors might be important in certain circumstances. For example the widespread distribution and continuous breeding of *An. gambiae s.l.* in the south, and more seasonal breeding in the north results in an endemic transmission pattern nationwide, with three distinct regions. In the coastal region of Benin, which has many lakes and lagoons, there are two vectors: *An. melas* and *An. gambiae s.l.* Above the coastal region, malaria is holoendemic, and *An. gambiae s.l.* is the vector. Finally, in northern Benin, malaria is normally seasonal, with a dry season (November to June) and a rainy season (July to October) during which malaria rates are highest. Recent entomological monitoring in 2012, and again in 2013[1], confirmed the presence of insecticide resistance among mosquito vector populations collected on the eastern side of one department where IRS is planned.

C. COUNTRY HEALTH SYSTEM DELIVERY STRUCTURE AND MINISTRY OF HEALTH ORGANIZATION

Administratively, Benin is divided into 12 departments (average of 650,000 inhabitants per department), 77 communes, 546 *arrondissements*, and 3,747 villages. There are three urban areas: Cotonou, Porto Novo and Parakou. Benin's public health system has a pyramid structure with three levels:

- Central: The MOH and its central Directorates; one National Referral Hospital (*Centre National Hospitalier Universitaire*);

- Intermediate: Departmental Directorates for Health, Departmental referral hospitals (*Centres Hospitaliers Départementaux*). There are only six functional tertiary referral hospitals nationwide; and

- Peripheral: Health zones, which include the following health facilities: Zonal hospitals (*Hôpitaux de Zone*), District Health Centers (*Centres de Santé de la Commune*), Community Health Centers (*Centres de Santé d'Arrondissement*), private health facilities, and village health units. In practice, not all health zones

---

[1]Africa Indoor Residual Spraying project. November 2012. *Semi-Annual Report, April-September 2012.* Bethesda, MD. Africa IRS project, Abt Associates Inc.

have a functional zonal hospital. The country's 34 health zones each cover an average population of 262,000 (ranging from 84,000 to 492,000). Health zones serve one to four communes (average of two communes per health zone).

Community health workers (CHWs)

Since 2009, over 8,000 CHWs with a primary education have been hired throughout Benin. They are supervised by the local health center and receive a quarterly stipend ranging from $20-30 depending on actual performance. There are two categories of CHWs. First, there are CHWs based in villages more than five kilometers from health facilities; they are trained to treat malaria with ACT. They typically serve approximately 30 households each. Second, there are CHWs who are based in villages less than five km from a health facility, who are trained mainly in health promotion activities and serve up to 50 households. Since the introduction of malaria treatment, the MOH has expanded the package to include other high impact interventions including essential newborn care, integrated treatment of diarrhea and pneumonia, and more recently family planning services. With these increased responsibilities and with challenges of CHW motivation, the MOH is planning to enhance the professional training of all CHWs as well as raise the minimum level of qualifications required for the position. A national forum is planned in July 2013 and is expected to establish new directives regarding the new role of the CHWs. With this new role for CHWs being planned, USAID/Benin is working in collaboration with the Maternal and Child Health (MCH) program to determine CHW needs in terms of initial and refresher training for malaria diagnosis and treatment and for improved reporting of commodities consumption data.

Private health providers

The private health sector in Benin is varied and includes traditional practitioners (all of whom are unlicensed), private hospitals run by faith-based organizations, private facilities run by licensed health practitioners, unregulated providers, and unlicensed drug vendors. According to the 2012 Benin Health Systems 20/20 assessment, health sector human resources in Benin number 18,078 people, 25% of which (approximately 4,500 people) are in the private sector. Formal registration of private practices with the MOH remains a major issue; a 2005 survey of 231 private providers found that only 12% were authorized to practice. The MOH is authorized by law to work with licensed facilities and practitioners, but not unlicensed ones. This is a potential obstacle, as the unauthorized private sector is an important source of care for the urban poor.

D. NATIONAL MALARIA CONTROL PLAN AND STRATEGY

Benin's National Strategic Plan for malaria was written in 2011 to cover the period 2011– 2015. With the changes during the last two years in malaria epidemiology, malaria control strategies and in the political and donor environments, the NMCP embarked on an update in 2012. The revised strategic plan was originally scheduled for ratification in April 2013, but this deadline has been delayed. The plan states a long-term vision to achieve a "Benin without malaria," and the goal is "to reduce Benin's malaria burden to a level that it will no longer be a roadblock to national socio-economic development." The strategic plan states its objective as follows: "By 2030, malaria will have been controlled and the trends in its incidence will have been reversed."

The priorities for the achievement of the strategy will not change and will continue to focus on:

- Preventive measures proven by effectiveness at the individual and community levels, e.g., sleeping under a long-lasting insecticide-treated mosquito net (LLIN), IRS with long-lasting insecticides, other anti-vector measures that reduce the contact between man and the mosquito vector, and the prevention of malaria among pregnant women;
- Early diagnosis and treatment with efficacious drugs of choice for all cases of malaria, including those at the community level;
- Community-based prevention, early diagnosis and treatment of all malaria cases;
- Integration of malaria control activities with primary health care and other development activities;
- Surveillance and M&E of interventions implemented to ensure that trustworthy strategic information is available;
- Operations research that will improve program performance;
- Capacity building and post-training follow-up for appropriate program implementation;
- Advocacy and behavior change communication; and
- Reinforcing partnerships to mobilize resources for malaria eradication.

Other supporting elements in the strategy include the following items under major themes:

Prevention
1. Integrated vector control – This approach will target both adult mosquitoes and larvae, when appropriate, with WHO Pesticide Evaluation Scheme (WHOPES)-approved insecticides, applying an environmentally sound methodology and universal LLIN coverage of the at-risk population. The resistance of known vectors to insecticides will be rigorously and routinely monitored.

2. Prevention of malaria in pregnancy (MIP) – This will include universal LLIN distribution and use, IPTp with sulfadoxine-pyrimethamine (SP) during antenatal visits beginning with the second and continuing into the third trimester.[2]
3. Prevention among specific groups, such as those with sickle-cell anemia and immigrants without immunity.

Diagnosis and clinical management

1. Diagnosis – This will be confirmed prior to treatment by either microscopy or a rapid diagnostic test (RDT). This will be rigorously applied for every suspected case of malaria at all levels of care and in the community. The proof of positive microscopy or RDT results will be required prior to the administration of ACT.
2. Treatment – ACTs (artemether-lumefantrine and artesunate-amodiaquine in Benin) are the drugs of choice for all cases of uncomplicated malaria, including cases at the community level. The use of oral artemisinin monotherapy is strictly forbidden by the WHO, a rule which Benin's MOH has adopted. For the treatment of simple malaria in pregnancy, oral quinine is recommended during the first trimester, while ACTs are recommended beginning with the second trimester. The use of rectal artesunate prior to referring a patient to the next level of care, if practical and acceptable, is recommended at the community level. Severe malaria is considered life-threatening, and its diagnosis should be confirmed. It should be managed at appropriately equipped health facilities and by trained and competent health professionals. The use of parenteral artesunate as first drug of choice for severe malaria is recommended; parenteral quinine is advised if artesunate is not available. As soon as the patient stabilizes, treatment should shift to oral medications.
3. Surveillance and pharmaco-vigilance – The sensitivity of malaria to recommended drugs will be monitored, and cases of resistance should be reported and investigated.
4. Private sector collaboration – This will be expanded to ensure that the growing number of private care providers align their diagnostic and therapeutic practices with national policies. This is strategically important due to the growing numbers of private clinics and practitioners who provide services to Benin's growing middle class.

Management of epidemics and complex humanitarian emergencies

---

[2] The details related to this section of the National Malaria Strategic Plan are being finalized.

The emergence of epidemics will be carefully monitored when large population movements occur, especially when the movement is from a non-endemic or low-endemic zone to an area of high exposure to malaria. The increased incidence of malnutrition may be associated with lower immunity and increased vulnerability.

Advocacy, behavior change communication, and social mobilization

Behavior change is essential for the increased uptake of healthy behaviors related to the prevention of malaria. Social mobilization is a major requirement in interrupting malaria transmission – from the implementation of universal LLIN distribution campaigns to the acceptance of new behaviors by households, health workers, and health personnel. Advocacy to garner political support and additional resources is necessary for the maintenance of programs.

Health systems strengthening and capacity building

The NMCP's strategic plan focuses on the following building blocks of the health system: better governance; adequate human resources – in absolute numbers, technical competence, and managerial capacity; financial resource mobilization; supply chain management; and partnerships, both public-private and international donor or technical partnerships.

Supply chain management

The NMCP is committed to work with the National Directorate for Pharmacy and Laboratories to ensure regulatory functions and compliance on malaria-related issues. Close coordination with the Central Medical Stores (CAME) is necessary for ensuring malaria medicines, products, and supplies are available to those who need them at the right time and in the right quantities. Different tools, including the LMIS, EUV survey, joint supervision visits, and weekly monitoring summaries, are in place to improve supply chain management.

Malaria surveillance and health information systems

The Routine Malaria Information System (RMIS) functions to detect epidemics and to serve as a barometer of efficacy of the current package of malaria interventions in reducing the national malaria burden. The NMCP uses the RBM/WHO-recommended indicators for monitoring national malaria programs. The strategic plan will be evaluated using accepted international norms and methodologies. The DHS and other surveys have been used to evaluate achievement of the strategic plan's targets and will continue to be used in the future. Operations research on malaria continue to test promising innovations that could help accelerate the achievement of national targets in access, coverage, utilization, and impact.

E. INTEGRATION, COLLABORATION AND COORDINATION

Benin's malaria stakeholders include government, civil society, the private sector, academia, and external donors. The MOH's NMCP, a unit of the National Directorate for Public Health *(Direction Nationale de la Santé Publique)*, is the government's recognized entity to ensure coordination and supervision of the country's malaria policy and program. Various civil society organizations act as implementing partners of the NMCP, especially at the community level and in remote areas where the MOH has little or no presence. Academia's role is to provide technical assistance and training. The private sector is represented by private clinics, individual service providers, commercial establishments, and vendors of goods and services that are used in malaria programs. External donors are foreign assistance providers like PMI, the Global Fund, the African Development Bank (AfDB), and the World Bank. Beginning in FY 2013, when the World Bank and the AfDB shifted to district-focused Results-Based Financing, PMI and the Global Fund became the principal external donors to the NMCP.

Relationships between the malaria stakeholders listed above are collegial and collaborative, and have been that way for several years. There continues to be adequate space in different fora to resolve issues of mutual concern and enough goodwill among stakeholders to resolve differences amicably.

Progress in relationships during the last year
During the past year, the national experience on the policy of providing free malaria services and products occupied the attention of the NMCP. The Minister of Health, Professor Dorothée Kinde-Gazard, a malariologist, authorized external monitoring visits and made field visits on her own to observe the application of the policy. The resulting recommendations, which were closely observed by partners, centered on the reimbursement from the national budget of malaria products and services incurred by health facilities. The NMCP was designated to verify the documents submitted prior to payment. A related issue that was focused on was the National Health Insurance System (*Regime d'Assurance Maladie Universelle* or RAMU), which had a "soft" launch using *mutuelles,* a form of community-based health insurance scheme. The RAMU aims to assure universal health coverage in Benin when fully functioning.

The following continue to act as platforms for better information-sharing, problem-solving, and harmonization of strategies and actions among Benin's malaria donors:

1. **NMCP as a hub for communication and coordination.** The NMCP is the designated hub for coordination of malaria activities in Benin. All technical working groups have met regularly over the past year, and the supply chain management working group has started meeting weekly to monitor and pre-empt stockouts. Stakeholders volunteer their time to the working groups, based on their expertise and the character of their portfolio. The NMCP annually holds the *Plan Intégré du Travail Annuel* (PITA) workshop to harmonize stakeholders' annual plans. This is meant to foster mutual information-sharing early in the planning process and ensure better coordination. However, the use of the PITA is not being maximized; gaps in the information provided by partners limit its usefulness as the principal reference document in malaria planning each year. With the new five-year strategic plan, there is a need to increase coherence in the shared targeting of long-term goals for elimination of malaria as a public health problem.

2. **Roll Back Malaria (RBM) Network.** The NMCP acts as the convenor of the RBM network in Benin. Most of the monthly meetings scheduled during the year took place as planned. The NMCP Coordinator is the chair. All stakeholders present are given the opportunity to report on their malaria activities during the previous month. This local RBM network is closely linked to the West Africa RBM Network (WARN) and the global RBM Network based in Geneva.

3. **The Country Coordinating Mechanism (CCM) for the Global Fund.** The CCM is an in-country group with the dual responsibilities of shepherding proposals to the Global Fund Secretariat in Geneva and providing oversight to the successful achievement of objectives of approved proposals. USAID/Benin serves as a permanent member of the CCM and is actively involved in the Malaria Working Group and in the Strategic Oversight Committee.

4. **The *Partenaires Techniques et Financiers (PTF)*.** The members of this group meet monthly and have quarterly retreats with the Minister of Health. They comprise the major external donors to Benin's health sector, with the exception of China, which imports large amounts of ACTs. While the group's interests extend beyond malaria, the group has been very supportive of health program-related reforms, such as PMI's support to the CAME. USAID/Benin sits as PTF Vice-Chair for the next two years.

5. **One-on-one coordination meetings.** These types of meetings are still the mainstay of coordination efforts in Benin. However, they are time-consuming and are disadvantageous to those partners that are based up-country and do not have offices in Cotonou.

6. **The Malaria Operational Planning (MOP) exercise.** The week-long annual visit of colleagues from the U.S. Centers for Disease Control and Prevention (CDC)/Atlanta and USAID/Washington is an excellent opportunity for sharing information, lessons learned, and experiences. The debates in the meetings, the group work, and presentations provide additional insights that enrich the PMI MOP.

F. PMI GOALS, TARGETS AND INDICATORS

In Benin, the goal of PMI is to reduce malaria-associated mortality by 70% compared to pre-initiative levels. Pre-initiative levels are those existing during the time period covered by the 2006 DHS. By the end of 2014, PMI will assist Benin to achieve the following targets nationwide, as the entire population is at risk for malaria:

- >90% of households with a pregnant woman and/or children under five years of age will own at least one ITN;
- 85% of children under five years of age will have slept under an ITN the previous night;
- 85% of pregnant women will have slept under an ITN the previous night;
- 85% of houses in geographic areas targeted for IRS will have been sprayed;
- 85% of pregnant women and children under five years of age will have slept under an ITN the previous night or in a house that has been protected by IRS;
- 85% of women who have completed a pregnancy in the last two years will have received two or more doses of IPTp during that pregnancy;
- 85% of government health facilities have ACTs available for treatment of uncomplicated malaria; and
- 85% of children under five years of age with suspected or confirmed malaria will have received treatment with ACTs within 24 hours of onset of their symptoms. (Note that with a policy of only treating patients with a positive malaria test this target is losing relevance. PMI is working with RBM to develop a better case management target.)

In July 2012, the Minister of Health directed the NMCP to achieve five bold malaria targets to be achieved by December 2012: (1) At least 80% of all children with fever receive appropriate care within 24 hours; (2) At least 80% of all clients receive correct case management of simple and severe malaria; (3) At least 80% of pregnant women are sleeping under an LLIN; (4) At least 80% of children under five are sleeping under an LLIN; and (5) At least 80% of all pregnant women receive two doses of IPTp. The NMCP has established specific work teams with its partners to achieve each of the five results and these previously established targets are still current and relevant.

G. PROGRESS ON COVERAGE AND IMPACT INDICATORS TO DATE

The table below presents estimates of malaria indicators. Most results were measured by the two most recent DHS's, which were nationally-representative household surveys. Estimates from the 2006 DHS, which was conducted from August–November 2006 (approximating the duration of the short rainy season), have been accepted as the baseline indicators for Benin. The 2012 DHS was conducted from December 2011– March 2012 (covering the dry season). The IRS indicator is current for 2012, and the data are from PMI program monitoring documents, rather than a DHS.

Table 1. Benin's Malaria Indicators

Indicator	2006 DHS	2012 DHS	2012 IRS monitoring report
Households with ≥ 1 ITN	25%	80%	
Children ≤ 5 years of age sleeping under an ITN the previous night	20%	70%	
Pregnant women who slept under an ITN the previous night	20%	75%	
Women who received ≥ 2 doses of IPTp during their last pregnancy in the last two years	< 1%	23%	
Children ≤ 5 years of age with fever in the last two weeks who received treatment with an ACT within 24 hours of fever onset	<1%	7%	
Houses targeted for IRS that were sprayed			95%

H. OTHER RELEVANT EVIDENCE ON PROGRESS

The level of awareness about malaria is very high in Benin. In a recent baseline survey for a PMI-funded operations research project through the Child Survival and Health Grants Program in the commune of Sémé-Kpodji (a mixed peri-urban and rural commune near Cotonou), demand for mosquito nets was very high. Mothers confronted the survey team to demand that more LLINs be sent to the commune for vulnerable mothers and their babies.

The high levels of knowledge of malaria among various groups have been due to behavior change campaigns supported by various malaria projects, including PMI. However, even beyond the campaigns, the media in Benin have been very supportive of the dissemination of malaria information. There are weekly health programs aired by different TV channels; at least one of them features malaria in any given month. Over the years, radio outlets - whether religious, commercial or community - have complemented other media in disseminating information on malaria prevention. Benin's print media, considered the liveliest in West Africa, also contribute to informing the public on malaria prevention.

I. CHALLENGES, OPPORTUNITIES, AND THREATS

Challenges

Malaria is a major burden on the population's health and economy in Benin. The 2012 DHS showed some progress in controlling the disease, but much more remains to be done before the objective of near-zero deaths due to malaria is achieved by 2015. Benin, like most developing countries, is plagued by the following challenges: (1) an acute health worker crisis - both in terms of absolute numbers and professional qualifications; (2) weak leadership and management skills of national, departmental and district supervisors; (3) a weak supply chain management system, especially at the health zone level where product stockouts and leakages are common; (4) a Health and Management Information System that is still developing protocols and methodologies, especially in routine monitoring and data quality; and (5) incomplete implementation of national policies and treatment protocols.

Although Benin is a small country, it is culturally diverse and linguistically complex, making communication of concepts and directives difficult, costly and time-consuming to implement. This is compounded by a large iliterate segment of the population: six out of ten adult women have never been to school. Implementing behavior change strategies at different levels requires effort and time. For example, it has been a major challenge over the past three years to ensure implementation of the national policy to treat malaria with ACTs only when the diagnosis is confirmed with an appropriate RDT or microscopy. Changes in health workers' attitudes to RDTs are finally being observed, but getting to this point has required more time and investments in training and supervision.

Other challenges include a growing private sector that needs to be more engaged in malaria control, a growing urban population with little access to organized health services, and a national policy environment that has not given health the appropriate level of priority in budget allocations. The 2012 proportion of the national budget allocated to health was 6.6%, well below the recommended level of 15% for sub-Saharan Africa, which Benin subscribed to in the Abuja Declaration of 2001

Opportunities

Despite the above challenges, Benin has made substantial progress in the past few years. The proposed revisions to Benin's new five-year NMCP strategy provide further clarity on the advancement of malaria control, enabling Benin to align activities with global RBM priorities. During the MOP design exercise, there was vigorous NMCP participation at all points of the process. There is a strong, collaborative partnership between the MOH and donors, which constitutes a solid platform for the elimination of malaria as a public health problem in Benin.

Decentralization of public sector health services is finally being embraced by the MOH as a vehicle for accelerating coverage of malaria and other programs. This has started to generate opportunities for many actors to collaborate actively beyond the MOH's central level. At the health zone and department levels, donors have collaborative arrangements around local health issues that give communities a voice. Decentralization also expands the pool of human resources that could be mobilized for behavior change and universal LLIN distribution campaigns.

The increased involvement of the private sector constitutes a major opportunity, especially because there are more households entering the middle class each year. With the launching of the private sector component of ARM3 in March 2013, there were more businesses enthusiastically embracing malaria control in Benin. The chief executive officer of the Bank of Africa had a major delegation attending the launch and declared that it makes good business sense for commercial enterprises to assist employees and their families in getting protected against malaria, HIV/AIDS, tuberculosis, and other preventable infections.

Threats
The lack of effective leadership, good management, and transparent governance within the NMCP and other MOH units represents a constant threat to the effectiveness and sustainability of malaria interventions. The few health workers who demonstrate technical and managerial competence are quickly recruited by international agencies and consulting firms. To ensure that activities undertaken by PMI continue beyond its period of support, the transfer of knowledge, capacity, and responsibilities to a strong NMCP and other government staff is vital. Currently, another threat to the NMCP has emerged; after a peak in 2010, there has been a gradual reduction in external financial resources for malaria. In 2011, the World Bank decided to shift its assistance to Benin's health sector to a performance-based funding arrangement with a limited number of health zones. The Global Fund has already reduced its contributions to the malaria program and has postponed any new proposals to 2014 under its New Funding Mechanism.

Aside from political and program issues, malaria vector-insecticide resistance threatens two of the four PMI interventions (ITNs and IRS). Resistance to pyrethroids, used on ITNs, has been shown to reduce impact[3]. Additionally, widespread vector resistance to two of the three approved classes of IRS insecticides has emerged (see IRS entomology monitoring section). The IRS issue is further complicated by the fact that the long-lasting formulations of the remaining insecticide class (the organophosphates, or o-ps), needed for

---

[3] N'Guessan *et al*. Reduced efficacy of insecticide-treated nets and indoor residual spraying for malaria control in pyrethroid resistance area, Benin. *Emerg Infect Dis* 2007
http://www.cdc.gov/EID/content/13/2/199.htm

IRS, are not approved by WHOPES and, consequently, will not be approved for use by the MOH.

J. PMI SUPPORT STRATEGY

Benin was selected as a PMI focus country in 2008, although large-scale implementation of ACTs and IPTp, and the large-scale distribution of ITNs began earlier in 2007 with the support of other partners like the World Bank and the Global Fund, in spite of the weak health infrastructure.

In the FY 2010 MOP, PMI decided to group the majority of activities under a single malaria bilateral project. Following an application and review process in FY 2011, a new five-year bilateral was awarded on October 3, 2011, titled Accelerating the Reduction of Malaria Morbidity and Mortality (ARM3). Certain elements, such as IRS and commodities procurement, remain centrally managed to ensure global standards are met and to benefit from the advantages of bulk purchasing via a central mechanism.

PMI staff work closely with ARM3 to ensure that all technical areas are covered in the work plan through consortium partners and sub-partnership networks. New ARM3 key personnel have recently been hired to provide additional support for the following technical areas: case management, supply chain management, BCC, and M&E. Specific milestones are listed in the cooperative agreement and work plan. These are based on MOP activities and are covered during the quarterly review.

PMI's support to Benin's NMCP covers the whole country, except for IRS which is focused on only one department in the north of the country. National-level support for FY 2014 includes:
  a) Continued routine distribution of ITNs through ANC and immunization clinics to pregnant women and children under five years of age, respectively, as well as a recently-added pilot school-based distribution in three departments;
  b) Improved malaria diagnostics and case management;
  c) Sustained support to the health information system, especially on routine monitoring and periodic evaluations;
  d) Improved pharmaceutical and commodity supply chain management; and
  e) Behavior change communication.

Capacity building and health system strengthening will focus on improving leadership, management, and governance of the NMCP as a functional unit within the MOH at the central level. Department-level malaria staff will be given the opportunity to build their capacity in malaria epidemiology. Current activities in community case management are implemented by ARM3, with funding from both PMI and USAID/Benin's Maternal and Child Health funding stream.

III. OPERATIONAL PLAN

A. PREVENTION

1. Insecticide-treated nets (ITNs)

Background:
The NMCP's National Plan is to achieve 90% coverage of pregnant women and children under five sleeping under ITNs. The strategy to achieve this coverage consists mainly of (i) large-scale routine distribution of ITNs to pregnant women and children under five years of age through antenatal and immunization clinic services, and (ii) triannual mass distribution campaigns, which provide free nets to all population groups (defined as one long-lasting insecticide-treated net for every two people) nationwide. Social marketing and school-based distributions of ITNs are complementary activities that contribute to the main distribution strategies.

In 2007, 1.6 million nets were distributed to children under five years of age during the first mass distribution campaign. The second campaign was conducted in July 2011. A total of 4,867,500 million nets were distributed by several partners: 55% of ITNs were provided by The Global Fund, 35% by the World Bank, 6% by PMI, and 4% by the ADB. While there was no gap for the 2011 campaign, Benin expects a gap of 16,866 nets in the 2014 campaign. Of the 6 million nets required in 2014, 5.9 million have been committed by the GOB and partners. PMI has committed 680,000 nets with FY 2013 funding. With the projected carry over of 632,471 nets from 2013, we hope that the 2014 gap will be covered.

The 2012 DHS found that a majority of all households (86%) owned at least one mosquito net of any type, 80% of households reported owning at least one ITN, and 70% of children under five years of age and 75% of pregnant women said that they had slept under an ITN the previous night. These data confirm significant progress in terms of ITN ownership and usage since the baseline in 2006, when ownership and usage levels were $\leq$25%.

Progress during the last 12 months:
Using FY 2011 funds, in 2012, PMI procured 510,000 ITNs for free routine distribution. Of the 510,000 ITNs, 385,000 will be distributed through ANC and immunization activities, while an additional 100,000 ITNs will be distributed through social marketing

in the private sector. Following the July 2011 mass distribution campaign, the MOH suspended routine distribution of nets. Routine distribution was re-initiated in May 2012. Due to this suspension, an estimated 205,000 ITNs remained as carry over to be distributed at health facilities in 2013.

Peace Corps Volunteers across the country observed that a number of pregnant women and children did not receive nets during the campaign and the routine service interruption. Peace Corps/Benin is developing local targeting plans with health centers and community-based organizations to distribute 25,000 to fill gaps in 75 communities throughout all 12 departments in Benin over the next 24 months. These nets arrived in February of 2013 and are being stored in Cotonou while the distribution protocols are finalized with the NMCP.

Finally, PMI continued to support and strengthen entomological monitoring and evaluation of PMI vector control interventions in partnership with the Center for Entomological Research – Cotonou *(Centre de Recherche Entomologique de Cotonou*, or CREC). A PMI operations research (OR) activity (further detailed in the OR section) to track ITN loss (i.e., removal from a house for any reason) following the universal campaign is underway using three WHO indicators: net survivorship, bio-efficacy, and durability. CREC has already completed an ITN retrospective tracking assessment, which examined nets distributed in 2007. Another assessment is ongoing.

Challenges, opportunities, and threats:
Routine distribution of ITNs is a strategy that has contributed to increased use of health services, especially ANC and immunization services. A new strategy of school-based distribution has been suggested by the NMCP, and will be piloted in CY 2014, following a recent training workshop on the NetCalc tool that incorporated this distribution channel. Using NetCalc as a planning tool may help Benin increase coverage in certain areas which could contribute to and sustain universal coverage of ITNs.

The school-based distribution strategy is one way to immediately increase ITN ownership. Several challenges to ITN scale-up include: (1) management of services in terms of planning, monitoring, and evaluation of the distribution; (2) availability of staff committed to those services; (3) proper care of ITNs; (4) management of pyrethroid resistance to insecticides used in ITNs; and (5) quality control and efficiency in use by the target group. A new threat is the growing evidence base that suggests that many ITNs develop holes in just the first six months of use[4].

---

[4] ITN loss / survivorship estimated according to *Guidelines for monitoring the durability of long-lasting insecticidal mosquito nets under operational conditions.* WHO/HTM/NTD/WHOPES/2011.5

USAID/Benin has supported ProFam, a network of 50 registered private for-profit clinics, since 2006. In 2011, these clinics provided 12,852 first antenatal care visits; however, since October 2011 with the closing of the IMPACT project that was the conduit for ProFam support, the clinics no longer receive subsidized nets for routine distribution. To fill this gap, PMI proposes to work with NMCP to re-initiate this service. The ITN needs have been quantifed in Table 2 below.

Table 2. ITN Gap Analysis for 2013-2016

A. Need and Funding Source[5]	2013	2014	2015	2016
Routine (pregnant women)	403,514	427,725	453,388	480,592
Routine (children under five)	286,015	303,292	321,390	340,344
Routine (school)		332,793[6]	633,421	654,007
Routine (ANC private sector ProFam)	13,000	13,650	14,333	15,049
Mass Distribution Campaign		5,542,623		
Total ITN need (A)	**702,529**	**6,620,083**	**1,422,532**	**1,489,992**
B. Distributed and Committed				
PMI-MOP FY12	700,000			
PMI-MOP FY13		680,000		
PMI-MOP FY14			800,000	
Government of Benin	125,000	50,000	75,000	100,000
Global Fund	0	5,245,272	0	0
Carry Over Nets	510,000[7]			
Total ITNs already distributed or committed (B)	**1,335,000**	**5,975,272**	**875,000**	**100,000**
(Gap)/Surplus (A-B)	**632,471**	**(644,811)**	**(547,532)**	**(1,389,992)**

Note: Gap analysis data based on population-based estimates provided by the NMCP.

Plan and justification:
PMI will continue to work closely with the NMCP and other RBM partners to support health system strengthening, through the improvement of supply chain management from the central level down to the health facilities, as well as forecasting, quantifying, tracking,

---

[5] Estimates are based on 2011 National Health Statistics report in regards to number of 1st ANC and 1st Immunuization clients at government health facilities and outreach services and ProFam 1st ANC clients with projected increase of 6% based on historical trend.

[6] Pilot of ITN distribution through schools will start in 3 departments in 2014 with plan to expand to all 6 departments in 2015.

[7] Routine distribution was suspended in 2011 due to the campaign, thus nets purchased by PMI with FY 2010 funding for routine services were distributed in 2012 instead. The 510,000 nets purchased with FY 2011 funding are being distributed through routine services in 2013.

and storage of malaria commodities including ITNs. PMI will also support the monitoring of vector resistance to insecticides (funds for this activity are outlined in IRS section). While the universal coverage campaign in 2014 is an important activity, the six percent (6%) that PMI will contribute is small compared to the total need, which will be covered by other partners.

Proposed activities with FY 2014 funding: ($3,600,000)

1. Procurement of long-lasting insecticide-treated nets (ITNs): Procure and ensure delivery of approximately 800,000 ITNs for routine distribution at government health facilities and 50 USAID/Benin supported ProFam clinics to pregnant women at ANC visits and children at immunization clinics. Pregnant women will receive one LLIN as part of a package during their first ANC visit. ($3,600,000)

2. Indoor residual spraying (IRS)

Background:
PMI is the only donor supporting IRS in Benin (the National Strategic Plan calls for IRS scale-up, but resources for expansion are lacking). Spraying began in 2008 in four communes in Ouémé Department in the South. However, the malaria transmission season in the region outlasted the duration of the IRS insecticidal effect, resulting in sub-optimal impact. Therefore, IRS was shifted (2011) to Atacora Department in the North, where the transmission season is shorter, requiring only one spraying campaign per year. Table 3 below summarizes the PMI contributions to the IRS program.

Table 3. PMI IRS rounds by date, location, coverage, and insecticide

Date month/year	Round	Region	Departme nt	Structures Sprayed	Population Protected	Insecticide
7-8/2008	1	South	Ouémé	142,813	521,698	carbamate
3-4/2009	2	South	Ouémé	156,223	512,491	carbamate
3-4/2010	3	South	Ouémé	166,910	636,448	carbamate
8-9/2010	4£	South	Ouémé	200,036	623,904	carbamate
5-6/2011	5£	North	Atacora	145,247	426,232	carbamate
5-6/2012	6	North	Atacora	210,380	652,777	carbamate
5-6/2013	7	North	Atacora	210,380*	652,777*	organophosphate (5 communes) carbamate (4 communes)

£ Indicates 3-4 months of effective life for carbamate insecticide (bendiocarb) applied by IRS during rounds 4 and 5.
*estimate based on 2012; actual figures not available until Q4 of 2013.

Long-standing evidence of vector (insecticide) resistance in West Africa[8] argued against the use of pyrethroid class insecticides in Benin. As a result, PMI has relied on carbamate-class insecticides for IRS since spraying began in 2008. However, IRS entomological monitoring in 2012[9], and again in 2013[10], confirmed the presence of vector resistance to carbamate-class insecticides in the IRS department.

---

[8] Chandre, F. *et al*. 1999.Status of pyrethroid resistance in *Anopheles gambiae* sensu lato. Bull. WHO 77(3):230.
[9] Centre de Recherche Entomologique de Cotonou. 2012. Entomological Monitoring-Evaluation in the department of Atacora 6 months after indoor residual spraying, Benin, West Africa.CREC/PMI/Abt-2012
[10] Africa Indoor Residual Spraying project. November 2012. *Semi-Annual Report April-September 2012*. Bethesda, MD. Africa IRS project, Abt Associates Inc.

Table 4. Carbamate susceptibility of *An. gambiae s.l.* populations collected in IRS communes, 2010 versus 2012: % mortality (number tested)

IRS communes	October 2010	July 2012	October 2012
Tanguiéta	95(95)	63(82)	63(106)
Natitingou	97(92)	62(84)	
Kouandé	98(42)	79(74)	79(90)
Matéri	98(94)	59(29)	59(73)
Pehunco	95(83)		79(101)

In contrast, vector susceptibility to the o-p class of insecticides in the same locations remained high (98-100%; n=592 vectors tested in 4 IRS communes) through 2012. Therefore, PMI, in consultation with the NMCP, began rotating to IRS with o-p insecticides during the 2013 spray round. In 2014, o-p insecticides should be used in all IRS target areas to optimize impact and better manage the spread and intensification of insecticide resistance. Increased funding for IRS is being proposed to support the higher cost of o-p spraying across the target region.

Progress during the last 12 months:
Impact data[11], collected before and after IRS round six (2012) in 5 communes (2 sites per commune), were compared with similar measurements taken in one IRS comparison control commune. The results indicated that insecticide bio-activity was short-lived, lasting only two months.

Table 5. Mortality rate *An. gambiae s.l.* after 30 minute exposure to IRS-treated walls/ WHO cone assay for insecticide bio-activity. IRS target area populations versus 'carbamate-susceptible'-colonized population

IRS area	Substrate	% mortality following IRS		
		+1 week	+1 month	+2 months
Tanguiéta	Cement	100 (100)	90(100)	51(96)
	Mud	100(100)	85(100)	46(94)

---

[11] Entomological Data to inform round three of indoor residual spraying (IRS) in the Department of Atacora, Benin,CREC/Abt Associates Inc. 2012

Natitingou	Cement	100(100)	85(100)	54(90)
	Mud	100(100)	66(97)	50(82)

Entomological inoculation rates, estimated to be on the order of one infective bite per person every two nights during the transmission season (post IRS) in Kopargo (control area), were so low as to be undetectable in IRS target areas (n=150 vectors tested/month for 3-4 months post IRS).

Challenges, opportunities, and threats:

Challenges

Vector resistance to carbamate insecticides: At one site, vector resistance to carbamates was first seen in 2011. This phenomenon was then observed at multiple sites in 2012[6]. Insecticide rotation to the o-p class of insecticides, recommended by WHO[12] and PMI[13], began in 2013 and should be universal in 2014. Unfortunately, no alternative class of approved public health insecticides is available to rotate to when o-p resistance appears (a likely outcome given its use in cotton cultivation). A strategic approach to rotation between classes of IRS insecticides for resistance management, informed by comprehensive monitoring to assess change in resistance levels (phenotypes, mechanisms, and intensity), based on the WHO Global Plan for Insecticide Resistance Management[12], is being discussed with the NMCP as a response measure to manage the problem, until alternative classes of insecticide are approved.

Approval of a long-lasting o-p formulation: Two 'public health' formulations of the IRS o-p insecticide exist on the market. The emulsifiable concentrate formulation lasts three to four months, whereas the capsule suspension formulation has perhaps two times the longevity[14] of the emulsifiable concentrate formulation. The capsule suspension formulation, however, awaits WHO approval (the MOH will not authorize 'pre-approval' use of the capsule suspension formulation). While the approved emulsifiable concentrate formulation remains effective for most of the transmission season, it begins to degrade after three to four months, possibly leaving a sub-lethal (for the vector) insecticide dose on IRS-treated walls. As pointed out earlier, this situation can increase selection pressure for resistance in late season vector populations. In contrast, the longer-lasting capsule suspension formulation is more likely to remain effective well into the low transmission season, and therefore play less of a role in selection for resistance.

---

[12]WHO Global Plan for Insecticide Resistance Management. 2012. www.who.int/entity/malaria/vector_control/ivm/gpirm
[13]PMI IRS Technical Guidance 2012
[14]PMI results (unpublished) from Ghana evaluation of pyrimiphos-methyl (capsule suspension formulation)

Opportunities

To measure the impact of IRS on clinical malaria: The timeline in Figure 1 compares the timing of the annual IRS round in Atacora (shown by the bottom line, followed by the number of communes sprayed) and surveys that measure malaria indicators (shown as either MIS IV or V). The relative timing of these activities presents an opportunity to assess the impact of IRS on clinical measures of malaria transmission (i.e., malaria parasite prevalence and anemia prevalence) collected during the surveys. The Surveys (MIS) span IRS rounds six and seven. Comparison of IRS commune survey results may provide a direct epidemiological measure of IRS impact when compared with similar survey data from the IRS control area, Kopargo. Of equal interest is the fact that similar comparisons may also indicate the impact of ITN coverage (universal) plus IRS (targeted in Atacora) versus ITNs alone (comparison commune without IRS). These low-cost assessments, based on secondary analyses of data already planned to be collected, could yield dividends in terms of assessing the cost-benefit of both ITNs and IRS in country.

Figure 1. IRS rounds and Malaria Indicator Surveys – Atacora Department, Benin

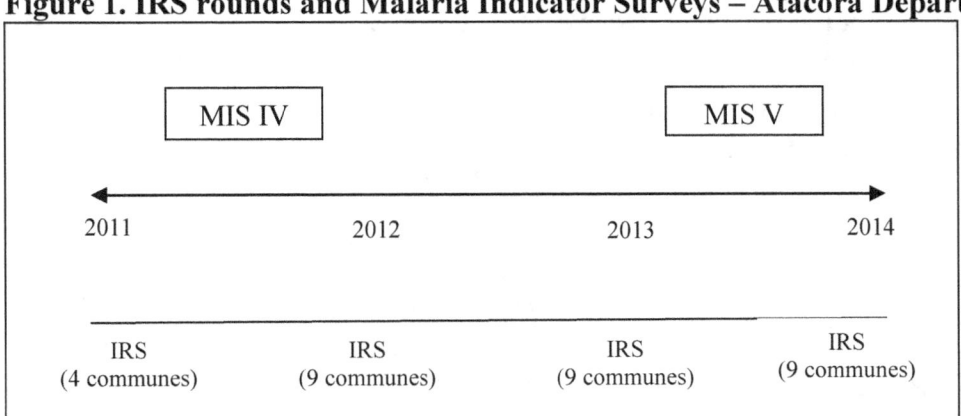

To build IRS capacity: The National Strategic Plan calls for expansion of IRS. However resources to support scale-up are lacking. After six years of PMI-supported IRS, Benin may be able to conduct independent IRS operations (like Madagascar, and other PMI countries), by attracting funds for insecticide and spray equipment from other sources and using PMI-trained spray personnel (department-level) to conduct IRS in parallel with PMI. The current PMI IRS partner is committed to developing national IRS capacity and, if supported, is willing to strengthen its mentoring program with the goal of having the national program conduct IRS in one new commune in 2015. Measures of IRS impact in the MOH-sprayed commune could be compared with results from PMI-supported IRS communes to confirm impact and safety. Objectives include: (1) strengthening of central capacity to plan, supervise, and support IRS; (2) strengthening of department-level capacity to operationalize IRS; (3) documentation of national competence in IRS to convince potential donors (insecticide and spray equipment) of the capacity to operationalize spraying. A short-term grant proposal to support the NMCP's IRS capacity has been submitted to WHO/TDR (Tropical Diseases Research) for potential funding.

Threats

Lack of national IRS ownership: Benin faces challenges related to malaria control. The ITN intervention, Benin's first-line malaria-vector control intervention, is threatened by malaria-vector insecticide resistance[15], probably as intense as anywhere in sub-Saharan Africa. There is a WHO plan[12] for responding to the resistance threat, which currently relies on the use of IRS with non-pyrethoid insecticides to manage the spread and intensification of pyrethroid resistance. Implementation of the plan in Benin should be a priority. Unfortunately, there appears to be little national 'appetite' for strategic planning around IRS. On a political level, the NMCP is deeply embedded in the MOH, often out of direct contact with the Minister, understaffed and under-resourced, given the severity of malaria in country. In terms of a national contribution to IRS, resources are scarce (Benin does not share in the natural wealth of, for example, its neighbor Nigeria). PMI can assist by building independent capacity to do IRS and by attracting donors interested in partnering with national and department-level programs that have experience (from prior PMI involvement) in the IRS intervention.

Plans and justification:

Annual, single-round IRS to reduce malaria transmission and manage resistance will continue in the nine communes of Atacora. Due to vector-insecticide resistance, spraying should be done with an o-p class insecticide. The FY 2014 budget has been increased to allow for the added cost of the new insecticide. A strategic plan for managing vector resistance will be developed to raise awareness of new WHO recommendations regarding rotation of IRS insecticide classes for the purpose of managing resistance and protecting ITN impact.

IRS entomological monitoring, conducted by CREC, will be done in accordance with the Benin IRS entomology monitoring and evaluation work plan. The plan provides for entomological surveillance at ten sites across Benin. Of these, six sites are dedicated to IRS impact evaluation, four in IRS areas, and two in non-IRS (comparison) areas. Four additional sites, located to the south of the IRS area, are also monitored to follow vector-insecticide susceptibility as it relates to the national ITN strategy.

---

[15] N'Guessan, R *et al.* (2007) Reduced Efficacy of Insecticide-treated Nets and Indoor Residual Spraying for Malaria Control in PyrethroidResisance Area, Benin.Emerg Infect Dis 13(2). Available from http://www.cdc.gov/EID/content/133/2/199.htm

Proposed activities with FY 2014 funding: ($4,153,200)

1. IRS implementation: The IRS plan for FY 2014 funds (round four in the North) will be repeated with a recommendation that only o-p class insecticides (ideally, the long-lasting capsule suspension formulation) be used. There will be one round of spraying, protecting approximately 210,000 houses in Atacora Department. PMI will also continue to support integrated training of spray operators and community mobilizers identified in collaboration with local physicians, heads of health posts, mayors, and village leaders. BCC efforts to promote acceptance of and compliance with IRS will precede the spray round. BCC efforts for IRS will be used to inform beneficiaries about the positive benefits of IRS in controlling and preventing malaria, the environmental and safety issues related to the use of insecticides for IRS, and the importance of continuing to use bed nets year-round. PMI will also assist the NMCP to develop an IRS plan. ($4,000,000).

2. Entomological monitoring in IRS spray areas and resistance sentinel sites: Annual IRS impact at six sites and vector-insecticide susceptibility monitoring at 10 sites (six IRS + four additional) will validate IRS impact, and map vector-insecticide resistance. Some additional M&E activities, as recommended in the new PMI IRS guidelines, will be carried out: (1) evaluations for the presence of physiological resistance mechanisms in the malaria vector (including mixed function oxidases, a mechanism that, if present, can be managed through the use of new ITN products), and (2) evaluations for 'target site modification' resistance mechanisms related to carbamate resistance (esterases, insensitive acetylcholinesterase (iAChE0)) to better inform the IRS insecticide rotation plan. ($120,000).

3. Technical assistance for vector control: A CDC entomologist will make two trips to the region. One trip will provide technical support to the NMCP and the IRS partner for development and evaluation of new (chemical methods) technology to monitor loss of residual insecticide levels on walls following IRS. A second trip will be used to transfer CDC technology for identification of vector-insecticide resistance mechanisms: bio-chemical assay tests for vector mixed function oxidase levels, recommended by PMI guidance. An additional $9,000 (added to the CDC IAA mechanism) is being requested for the purchase of supplies, equipment, and reagents that are otherwise difficult to obtain in Benin. These include: reagents for detection of malaria infections in vectors - routinely supplied for measuring vector-parasite-infection levels ($1,000); reagents and equipment for gas chromatography-based measurement of insecticide residue levels on walls following IRS ($4,000); purchase/construction of 'high efficiency' back pack aspirators for collection of vectors during IRS entomological monitoring ($3,000); supplies and reagents for CDC bottle test vector-insecticide resistance testing ($1,000) ($24,200 (TA) + $9,000 (CDC/Entomology Branch support) ($33,200)

3. Malaria in Pregnancy (MIP)

Background:

The NMCP has adopted a multi-pronged approach to MIP. This approach promotes: free distribution of sulfadoxine-pyrimethamine (SP); free distribution of ITNs to pregnant women at their first ANC clinic visit; and first-line treatment of simple malaria in pregnancy with oral quinine during the first trimester, and artemisinin-based combination therapy (ACTs) beginning in the second trimester. For severe malaria in pregnancy, quinine is recommended during all trimesters. In November 2004, the NMCP adopted intermittent preventive treatment of malaria during pregnancy (IPTp) as a national policy, requiring that pregnant women receive two doses of SP, with HIV-seropositive women receiving daily cotrimoxazole prophylaxis. In 2005, the NMCP officially introduced IPTp as part of a comprehensive ANC package in all 12 departments.

The ANC package contains two doses of SP and an ITN, free of charge. For a cost of approximately $1, the woman can receive the remaining items of the package, which include iron supplements, 5 mg of folic acid, and mebendazole. In early 2013, the NMCP adopted an interim policy of at least two doses of SP starting during the second trimester of pregnancy and repeated any time until delivery. A third dose may be given up to the time of delivery. It is recommended that all doses of SP are administered under direct observation. WHO's current recommendation is for pregnant women to receive at least 3 doses of SP during pregnancy starting after twelve weeks of pregnancy until delivery, that HIV seropositive women receive daily cotrimoxazole, and a folic acid dose of 0.4 mg. In February 2013, the NMCP held a workshop to revise its MIP policy in accordance with WHO recommendations. However, the draft developed does not fully comply with the updated WHO recommendations, and states that pregnant women receive at least 2 doses of SP until delivery. Details implementing these recommendations are not finalized and discussions with NMCP, stakeholders and the MOH will continue.

Results from the 2012 DHS showed that ANC attendance in Benin is high. Specifically, 86% of pregnant women made at least one ANC clinic visit. Attendance rates are higher in urban compared to rural areas (91% vs. 82%, respectively). Due to the high level of multiple ANC visits, pregnant women attend their first ANC clinic visit relatively early in their pregnancy, at 4.2 months.

Despite the high ANC attendance rates, the 2012 DHS reported that the proportion of pregnant women who received two doses of SP during their last pregnancy in the last two years was 23%. This rate, although a significant increase from the 2006 DHS rate of <1% (prior to IPTp scale-up), is still below the PMI target of 85%. However, according to the NMCP, it is rare for pregnant women to complete more than two ANC visits due to cultural factors. PMI is supporting a rapid assessment to identify those factors. Findings from this assessment will contribute to developing an appropriate strategy and training programs to increase ANC attendance and boost IPTp coverage.

Progress during the last 12 months:
During the past 12 months, WHO updated its policy recommendation on MIP. Results of a meta-analysis of seven randomized trials among pregnant women in Africa provided definitive evidence of the benefit of increased birth weight of newborns when pregnant women received three or more doses of SP throughout their pregnancy.PMI has worked collaboratively with the Clinical Case Management Technical Working Group and NMCP to continue discussions of incorporating the updated WHO IPTp guidelines into the national strategy.

Additional efforts to scale up IPTp included upgrading the skills of government and private health workers through curriculum modifications at major training institutions. To train health workers on how to provide quality client counseling related to IPTp, the first draft of a training of trainer's manual on interpersonal communication was developed. Additionally, PMI supported improved supervision to health workers in all the 34 health zones to follow IPTp case management and prevention guidelines, in the context of focused-antenatal care. Several behavior change communication (BCC) campaigns were organized to promote IPTp and the use of ITNs, and 100,000 flyers were distributed to pregnant women during ANC services.

PMI supported the NMCP and the Case Management Technical Working Group to modify the integrated supervision tool to include a section for the collection of IPTp data to help verify if the second SP dose was received by women who gave birth as opposed to the number of women visiting the ANC clinic during the previous month. PMI delivered 1,050,000 doses of SP, which will cover all public and private sector needs for 2013.

Challenges, opportunities and threats:
Despite the increase of IPTp coverage according to the 2012 DHS, the proportion of women who received at least two doses of SP during their pregnancy remains relatively low in Benin. Key barriers seem to be the lack of awareness of the benefits of SP, negative beliefs about SP safety, and logistical bottlenecks resulting in stockouts at health facilities. Given Benin's low uptake of two SP doses, revising the national policy to include the latest WHO IPTp recommendations of administering at least three doses up until birth is under discussion by the Case Management Technical Working Group. These new recommendations may provide the opportunity and incentive to strategize rigorous IPTp two-dose scale-up interventions.

Plans and justifications:

With FY 2014 funding, PMI will focus its efforts on procuring SP, increasing IPTp uptake through the private sector, strengthening communications around IPTp with specific messaging, and improving the performance of health workers who provide routine ANC services.

Proposed activities with FY 2014 funding: ($124,000)

1. Procure sulfadoxine-pyrimethamine (SP): Procure 1,050,000 doses of SP to cover 2014 needs of an estimated 525,000 pregnancies. Doses will be available in the public and private sectors according to national policy. ($124,000); and

2. Provide support for supervision and refresher training of health workers in IPTp to improve quality of service: PMI will continue to support on-site supervision and refresher training for public and private health facility midwives and nurses to correctly deliver SP in the context of the focused antenatal care approach. Training will include benchmark assessments, on-the-job training of the new treatment algorithm, and coaching. Supervision will continue to be part of an integrated approach for supervision at health facilities. (Costs covered in Case Management-Treatment section).

B. CASE MANAGEMENT

1. Diagnostics

Background:

Effective case management of malaria depends on early, accurate diagnosis with microscopy or RDTs, followed by prompt, appropriate treatment. In February 2011, the NMCP updated their malaria case management guidelines to align them with WHO standards, recommending universal diagnostic testing for malaria. All patients with suspected malaria should be tested using microscopy or an RDT, including children under five years of age; and treatment decisions should be based on test results. Since then, PMI has supported widespread dissemination of this policy. The current malaria policy includes the use of RDTs throughout the health system, and RDTs are often the only diagnostic test performed at the peripheral level. Although testing is recommended for all malaria suspected cases, including at the community level, relatively few CHWs are trained to use RDTs. CHW training on RDTs has been delayed because an adequate supply of RDTs for CHWs has not yet been ensured. NMCP envisions scaling-up the use of RDTs by the CHWs in 2013. The implementation of the new recommendation on universal testing and the use of RDTs by CHWs will result in an increased demand for RDTs.

In general, implementation of testing policy has been challenging. Routinely collected health facility data during 2012 showed that 88% of patients with suspected malaria were rapidly or diagnostically tested for malarial infection. A health facility survey in a nationally-representative sample of 128 health centers in April 2012 showed that 24% of health facilities had a stockout of RDTs for more than three days in the past three months, only 39% of facilities had an updated stock card on RDTs, and only 28% of uncomplicated malaria cases had been diagnosed by microscopy or an RDT (i.e., most malaria diagnoses were based only on clinical signs and symptoms).

Table 4. RDT Gap Analysis for 2013–2016

Year		2013	2014	2015	2016
Total estimated RDT need (A)		**2,797,333**	**2,991,592**	**2,961,882**	**2,845,327**
GOB and Donors' Stated Commitments	Government of Benin	100,000	100,000	100,000	100,000
	Global Fund/RCC FM/Africare	317,242	402,096	342,506	-
	Global Fund/Round 7/CRS	256,779	300,773	495,158	-
	USG/PMI	1,000,000	1,500,000	1,700,000	1,500,000
	UNICEF	84,000			
	World Bank	1,060,000	1,060,000		
Carry Over RDTs		490,000			
Total RDTs available (B)		**3,308,021**	**3,362,869**	**2,637,664**	**1,600,000**
(Gap)/Surplus (A-B)		**510,688**	**371,277**	**(324,218)**	**(1,245,327)**

Note: Gap analysis data based on population-based estimates provided by the NMCP

The estimated need for RDTs for 2015 is 2,961,882 tests (see Table 4). With FY 2014 funding, PMI will purchase 1,700,000 RDTs to cover the country's gap. Microscopy is supposed to be available in hospitals and larger health facilities. The NMCP estimates that Benin needs an additional 129 microscopes to cover departmental hospitals, health zones, and commune health centers through 2015. The need for microscopes is defined by the NMCP as a minimum of two microscopes for every departmental and health zone hospital and one microscope for every commune health center. In 2009, the World Bank purchased 10 microscopes. Since 2008, PMI has purchased 65 microscopes and microscopy reagents. Thus, over half (58%) of the NMCP's need has been met.

PMI continues to support a comprehensive diagnostics strengthening program that involves the training of clinicians and laboratory technicians, the implementation of a quality control and quality assurance system, and strengthening supervision to ensure that health workers follow clinical practice guidelines. Despite progress in improving laboratory worker skills and diagnostic performance, efforts need to be maintained in training and formative supervision for health providers. PMI is placing an emphasis on the regular collection and reporting of reasonably valid monitoring data to assess key health facility indicators that measure the availability of commodities (e.g. RDTs), the appropriate use of diagnostic testing and antimalarials, and the frequency of supervisory visits for health workers. It is not clear, however, if this information is being gathered throughout the health information system. Therefore, PMI will make certain that "improvement of health information and data" is included in its implementing partner's work plan.

Progress during the last 12 months:
During the past year, supervision visits to maintain and improve quality microscopy and RDT diagnoses were conducted in 118 health facilities (90% were public facilities and 10% were private). Supervision was semi-annual for 72 of the facilities and quarterly for 46 facilities. Quality scores were 86% for slide preparation and 88% for slide reading. Despite the progress made in malaria diagnosis, 32% of health facilities are still prescribing antimalarial drugs to patients who have a negative RDT or microscopy result according to the health facility survey completed in April 2012. PMI will continue to work collaboratively with the National Referral Laboratory and the NMCP to improve confidence among health professionals in diagnostic testing and the appropriate use of test results when prescribing. This support will include training and supervision of laboratory technicians and the development of a quality assurance/quality control system.

PMI/Benin purchased 1,500,000 RDTs to cover needs for 2014 and basic materials for the maintance and repairs needed for the existing microscopes. In addition, 118 advanced user guides for the laboratory diagnosis of malaria will be developed and disseminated to health facilities.

Challenges, opportunities, and threats:
While building demand for RDTs, as per the revised national directive for case management of children under five, Benin is confronted with a funding and logistics challenge to rapidly train and equip CHWs to use RDTs. Further, the private sector is a growing and an increasingly important source for health care in Benin, therefore it will be important to ensure supervision and quality control of diagnostics at these sites. Currently, only accredited private facilities receive this support from the MOH. There is some uncertainty about the extent of the Global Fund's contribution to malaria

commodities, including RDTs, with the new funding model that has been recently launched.

Plans and justification:
To contribute to improved diagnostics, PMI's plan with FY 2014 funding is to help fill the gap of RDTs and microscopes and continue supportive supervision and quality controls of malaria diagnostics.

Proposed activities with FY 2014 funding: ($1,355,000)

1. Procure rapid diagnostic tests (RDTs): The estimated need for RDTs for calendar year 2015 is 2,961,882 RDTs. With FY 2014 funds, PMI will only plan on providing 1.7 million RDTs toward filling this gap. Additionally, recognizing that the estimated needs for RDTs (and other commodities, such as ACTs) are imprecise, PMI will remain flexible about purchasing commodities and might reprogram some of the funds to purchase more or less RDTs and ACTs, depending on ongoing assessments. PMI will work with the NMCP and other partners to clarify the true need, better understand RDT usage patterns, and ensure that supplies do not exceed demand. ($1,110,000);

2. Procure microscopes and laboratory reagents: Procure 15 microscopes and laboratory reagents. ($45,000); and

3. Support supervision and strengthening of malaria diagnostic activities: This activity focuses primarily on laboratory workers. Training is provided during supervision visits, with feedback given directly and individually to workers, emphasizing implementing policies and standard operating procedures, microscope maintenance, and quality control of slides/RDTs. There is a focus on enhanced outreach training to improve skills of health workers and to support supervision that improves the national malaria Quality Assurance/Quality Control (QA/QC) program for laboratory and clinical health workers. ($200,000).

2. Treatment

Background:
In 2011, the NMCP updated its malaria case management guidelines to recommend universal diagnostic testing for malaria, including the private sector and among CHWs. Artemether-lumefantrine (AL) remains the first-line treatment for uncomplicated malaria in Benin. Artesunate-amodiaquine (AS-AQ) is recommended for patients under six months of age, for those who cannot tolerate AL, and when AL is not available. Artemisinin-based combination therapies are available in the regional and health zone warehouses throughout the country and health staff have been trained to correctly treat

malaria since 2008. According to the latest health facility survey (April 2012), only 26% of health facilities visited had all the presentations of AL.

The free malaria treatment policy was launched in October 2011 for children under five years of age and for pregnant women. This is now largely in place in public health clinics; however, implementation is lacking in hospitals, the private sector, and at the community level. The main issues raised by this policy are the renewal of ACT stocks, the high cost of treatment of severe and complicated malaria and reimbursement of the cost of service delivery, including the drugs, to health facilities by the GOB after verification of diagnostic and drug registers. The reimbursement process is very slow, thus most health facilities complain of the limited funds available for the renewal of ACT stocks. In collaboration with other donors, PMI continues to provide training on the treatment protocol for uncomplicated malaria to service providers in the public and private sectors and continues to support supervision of uncomplicated malaria treatment at the outpatient level.

To support the integration of malaria case management into the broader arena of treating childhood illnesses, PMI has supported refresher training and formative supervision of 1,500 health facility workers in Integrated Management of Childhood Illness (IMCI).

The NMCP policy recommends treating severe malaria with quinine. Injectable artesunate or artesunate suppositories are recommended for pre-referral treatment of severe malaria. For pregnant women, although not all malaria cases are severe, the national guidelines consider them as urgent to underscore the importance of treating these cases. The recommended treatment depends on the trimester of pregnancy. For uncomplicated malaria during the first trimester, quinine is recommended; and ACTs are the drugs of choice during the second and third trimesters. For severe malaria, quinine is recommended regardless of the pregnancy term. Severely ill cases identified in peripheral outpatient health facilities should be referred to a larger health facility with an inpatient ward.

At the community level, PMI supports the Integrated Community Case Management (iCCM) of childhood illness including malaria, diarrhea, malnutrition and pneumonia. CHWs are being trained to manage uncomplicated malaria cases and to refer children with complicated malaria. The MOH has developed national guidelines for community health promotion by clarifying roles and responsibilities of different actors including the CHWs. According to these guidelines, CHWs can treat uncomplicated malaria with ACTs at the community level and refer severe cases to health facilities. The policy recommends testing all suspected cases of malaria before treatment. Most CHWs are trained in uncomplicated malaria treatment with ACTs but roll out of RDT training has been delayed due to insufficient RDT stocks.

The 2012 DHS found that only 7% of children under five with fever in the preceding two weeks were treated with an ACT within 24 hours of onset of symptoms. This value is only slightly higher than the baseline of <1% from the 2006 DHS. Possible causes of this result include: decreased care-seeking, poor treatment quality for children who are brought to a health worker, ACT stockouts, and mis-use of diagnostic testing (as according to case management guidelines, only children with a confirmed positive test should receive an antimalarial). A review of the final 2012 DHS results, along with some field visits, should reveal the causes of the low value for the treatment indicator.

Progress during the last 12 months:
The private sector accounts for a significant proportion of health facilities in Benin, and it is growing. Therefore, it cannot be overlooked in the fight against malaria. During the past year, 542 private sector health providers were trained in the new malaria policy. To this end, PMI, with the support of the NMCP, developed four training modules including: a training manual; a participating nurse's manual; a participating doctor's manual; and an orientation manual for pharmacists on the new malaria control policy. Two thousand new malaria case management policy manuals have been produced and disseminated countrywide.

Approximately 1.5 million ACT treatments will have been procured in several shipments for older children and adults. On-site supervision of health workers has been supported, including benchmark assessments, on-the-spot training on the new algorithm, coaching (including supervision of diagnostic activities), and training on the management of severe malaria.

Challenges, opportunities, and threats:
With the roll-out of iCCM of sick children and the integration of RDTs, the treatment of confirmed malaria among infants less than six months is now feasible in Benin. The NMCP is committed to introduce AL to CHWs in high-mortality health zones with low access to formal health services. At the same time, according to the 2012 DHS, timely care seeking for children with fever is very low and data from the BASICS midterm survey suggested preferential treatment of male children. Factors that may contribute to the lower than expected levels of ACT consumption following the national introduction of case management by CHWs, need to be assessed. They will likely include ACT supply problems, acceptability of the selected CHWs, and household decision-making behaviors. The availability of consumption data for forecasting is a major goal of the supply chain management improvement effort by PMI in Benin.

Public-private partnerships need to be strengthened to ensure that the largely unregulated private sector receives supportive supervision. There is growing commitment by the NMCP to be more inclusive of the private sector and to overcome policy barriers to collaboration.

Plans and justification:
MI's plan with FY 2014 funding is to continue to support filling the ACT supply gap, supply chain management, in-service IMCI training, supportive supervision, and to assist the NMCP to integrate treatment of confirmed malaria among infants less than six months of age, and widen the scope of the planned private sector assessment to include a focus on malaria case management.

Table 5: ACT Gap Analysis for 2013-2016

Year		2013	2014	2015	2016
Total estimated ACT need (A)		**2,566,964**	**2,241,752**	**2,023,953**	**2,289,026**
GOB and Donors' Stated Commitments	Government of Benin	200,000	100,000	75,000	75,000
	Global Fund/RCC FM/Africare	661,485	552,199	399,767	
	Global Fund/Round 7/CRS	431,250	583,174	495,158	
	USG/PMI	2,600,000*	1,500,000**	1,500,000***	1,023,180****
	UNICEF	60,000			
	World Bank	590,000	590,000		
Total ACTs available (B)		**4,542,735**	**3,325,373**	**2,469,925**	**1,098,180**
(Gap)/Surplus (A-B)		**1,975,771**	**1,083,621**	**445,972**	**(1,190,846)**

Note: Gap analysis data based on population-based estimates provided by the NMCP
*Quantities funded with FY 2012 funding
**Quantities funded with FY 2013 funding
***Quantities proposed for FY 2014 funding
****Quantities proposed for FY 2015 funding

Proposed activities with FY 2014 funding: ($3,600,000)

1. Procure artemisinin-based combination treatments (ACTs): For artemether-lumefantrine (AL), procure approximately 1.5 million treatments.

It is important to note that the gap analyses are based on population estimates and the surplus observed is theoretical and accounts for current challenges with commodities management, such as stockouts, over-supply, and the difficulties to get consumption data. The Supply Chain TWG is still actively pursuing consumption data to revise the gap analysis and is focused on improving stock management. The different tools, including the LMIS, EUV, joint supervision visits and weekly monitoring summaries of the Supply Chain TWG, are in place to improve supply chain management and help us to mitigate theft and expiry. ($2,100,000);

2. Support subsidization of severe malaria treatment: As part of the new national policy to provide free severe malaria treatment to children under five and pregnant women, PMI will provide subsidies to selected facilities. Such facilities will be selected based on the following criteria: (1) the presence of trained staff in case management of severe malaria, emergency triage, and urgent treatment strategies; (2) the absence or lack of sufficient equipment or supplies to support case stabilization; (3) a history of consistent data reporting and good performance. Under the leadership of the NMCP, donors need to better coordinate their joint efforts. The World Bank has committed to provide support to eight health zones. Treatment costs for severe malaria range from $42 per child under five to $52 per pregnant woman. ($200,000);

3. Support quality improvement and supervision of health workers at the facility level: Support supervisory visits, as part of a comprehensive quality assurance approach, to ensure high quality malaria case management with ACTs, focused ANC (which includes IPTp and ITN distribution), and the distribution of ITNs during routine immunization clinics. The quality assurance and quality improvement component of this activity will include improvement at the health facility level, as well as community involvement in health and oversight in health center management. The system, which will be coordinated with the MOH, will incorporate training of supervisors (including those responsible for supervising the CHWs that distribute ACTs), developing practical tools, supporting travel, conducting on-the-job observation and training, monitoring, and promoting correct use of diagnostic results. The training will also reinforce appropriate treatment, providing feedback, collecting, analyzing and using data to improve planning and training, motivating supervisors and workers, and will train supervisors to implement changes identified during supervision. The focus of supervision will be at the health facility, as the rollout of CHW programs is being covered by the Global Fund and through community-based PMI implementing partners. Technical experts from the MOH and PMI will provide oversight for this activity. The key goals are to: (1) provide supervision to at least 90% of health workers nationwide with malaria-related responsibilities at least once every three months; (2) ensure that at least 90% of patients needing malaria testing are tested; (3) ensure that at least 90% of patients (all ages) needing an antimalarial receive an effective treatment; and (4) ensure that at least 90% of patients (all ages) not needing an antimalarial do not receive one. Progress in reaching each of these four goals will be quantitatively monitored and reported every three to six months. These activities will be evaluated with monitoring data (based on supervisors' reports), health facility surveys, and the EUV tool, which will be implemented quarterly. ($500,000);

4. Support malaria training for health workers: Support training of health workers on new case management guidelines, which will target outpatient health facilities. This will address a gap of 750 in the number of trained health facility workers ($150,000);

5. Support IMCI training: Support in-service training of health workers in iCCM to maintain practice standards and prevent gaps in knowledge or performance. ($100,000);

6. Support community case management of malaria, pneumonia, and diarrhea: Support community case management of malaria, which will ensure AL distribution by CHWs targeting children under five, focusing on eight USG health zones with existing networks of trained CHWs and expanding into two underserved urban zones. These eight USG zones which have been identified with the NMCP and MCH Directorate have existing CHW networks that are different from those supported by the Global Fund. However, as these zones require strengthening, and suffer from low access to healthcare and high mortality rates, they are geographically the same zones and so receive complementary support for community organization activities. All CHWs in the ten zones will receive training in RDT use as part of the iCCM support package. These Global Fund resources will be combined with other USAID funding streams to ensure the comprehensive iCCM package is delivered, not just the malaria component. ($400,000);

7. Provide technical assistance for community case management of malaria, pneumonia, and diarrhea: Technical assistance to local NGOs implementing iCCM in five health zones, which complements the Global Fund iCCM program for malaria. ($150,000).

3. Pharmaceutical Management

Background:
The National Malaria Control Plan and Strategy contains goals for the supply, distribution, and management of drugs and products for malaria prevention and control with the following objectives:

- Facilitate the purchase of ACTs, SP, ITNs, and RDTs as needed
- Streamline spending
- Ensure sustainable distribution of essential products to support malaria prevention
- Improve inventory management

- Encourage proper use of drugs and ITNs
- Monitor/evaluate the process of purchasing and distribution
- Measure the performance of supply and distribution

The Central Medical Stores (CAME) is the entry point for commodities into the pharmaceutical system. CAME recently finalized a strategy document, CAME Strategic Development Project Plan. The plan outlines CAME's strategic focus over the next five years, including an assessment of its human resource and financial needs. It also defines how CAME will improve distribution and warehousing, with a focus on better geographic distribution through the use of regional warehouses. CAME's goals for the period 2012 to 2016 are as follows:

- Improve conditions for product storage and for personnel
- Improve personnel management
- Ensure effective and continuous availability of pharmaceuticals
- Ensure the quality of medicines to the people served
- Improve the quality of customer service
- Improve CAME's visibility

Progress during the last 12 months:
Over the past 12 months, PMI continued to focus on the reform process at CAME. PMI provided support to train CAME's Board of Directors in good governance and strategic monitoring. Training topics included strategic monitoring, tendering and bidding procedures, M&E, risk analysis and management and the importance of strategic information for decision-making. In addition, PMI provided technical assistance to CAME to carry out an analysis of CAME's entire pharmaceutical stock, and to provide recommendations on how to improve health commodity storage. In addition to providing technical assistance to conduct the analysis, CAME personnel were trained on how to conduct similar analyses in the future for continued performance improvement and to increase the efficiency of CAME's operations.

In 2012, PMI provided assistance to CAME to improve the use of its information system. CAME installed new software (SAGE 100) that would allow it to access the stock status at its three warehouses (Cotonou, Parakou, and Natitingou). However, initially, CAME was not using the full functionality of the system to monitor stocks in real time. As a consequence, some warehouses were stocked out while others were overstocked. PMI provided technical assistance to improve CAME's use of the software to allow real time access to stock status of all three of CAME's warehouses. As a result, from the central level, all CAME warehouses can now be accessed in real time and adjustments can be made accordingly.

The above assistance to CAME resulted in real progress in the company's organization, professionalism, transparency, and its ability to deliver commodities in a timely manner.

Table 6 illustrates the importance of CAME's financial management capacity and expertise in the procurement of 174 orders of pharmaceuticals in 2012.

Table 6. CAME's financial management capacity, 2012

Type of procurement	Value in US $	Relative percentage
Tenders and restricted consultation	12,960,101	80,87%
Direct purchase of goods monopoly	1,478,113	9,22%
Direct purchase by wielding control	1,454,722	9,08%
Purchase with payment after sales	133,439	0,83%
Total	**16,026,375**	**100%**

Source: 2012 CAME Management Report

The CAME 2012 Management Report notes significant improvements in some key performance indicators regarding the procurement and distribution of commodities. The most notable are: stockout rate of 20% in 2010 vs. 12% in 2012; availability rate of tracer products of 80% in 2010 vs. 95% in 2012; expired goods rate of 1.50% in 2010 vs. 0.76% in 2012; and satisfaction rate of customer purchase orders of 80% in 2010 vs. 88% in 2012.

In collaboration with key partners and stakeholders, PMI provided support to the NMCP to redesign and harmonize the malaria Logistics Management Information System (LMIS). Through coordination meetings, partners and stakeholders identified four different information systems, each with their own reporting tools. Despite these systems being in place, the NMCP was still unable to track malaria commodities or obtain consumption data. Systems in place were partner specific, with information only being sent to implementing partners as opposed to the NMCP. In efforts to improve LMIS reporting, PMI provided support to NMCP to re-design and harmonize LMIS reporting tools. These new reporting tools were provided to all 34 health zones, 6 departmental hospitals (CHD) and 27 zonal hospitals. Following the re-design of the LMIS reporting tools, PMI provided support to train 96 health facility personnel on how to use the new LMIS tools. In addition, 34 health zone managers were trained to provide supportive supervision to newly trained staff.

Challenges, opportunities, and threats:

Although there have been substantial investments in the supply chain management system over the past five years, Benin continues to show weaknesses in its pharmaceutical management system. This is in part due to parallel commodity management systems across malaria partners. In addition, duplicative and uncoordinated reporting systems have resulted in the absence of reliable malaria commodity consumption data. As a result of this lack of data, chronic shortages, stockouts and overstocks continue to be major challenges. The redesigned LMIS, renewed efforts to improve coordination and the establishment of the logistics management unit will provide opportunities to strengthen Benin's supply chain management system.

Plans and justifications:

With FY 2014 funding, PMI will continue to build on the efforts recorded over the last few years to construct a more sustainable logistics and supply chain management system by implementing a set of targeted interventions. PMI's contribution will focus on capacity building for the pharmaceutical and supply chain management systems. In collaboration with other stakeholders, PMI will support strengthening of malaria supply chain management down to the facility level, strengthen the LMIS, and monitor the storage and distribution of malaria commodities. In addition to periodic evaluations of antimalarial efficacy, PMI will support antimalarial testing.

Proposed activities with FY 2014 funding: ($853,700)

1. Strengthen logistics management information system and supply chain management:
Continue to support and strengthen the national LMIS as well as the supply chain management system from the central level down to the health facilities. The proposed budget will be ($550,000) and includes the following specific activities:

- Strengthen logistics management information system and supply chain management through the reinforcement of the redesigned and harmonized LMIS, which includes the renewal of the Medistock license
- Provide technical assistance to CAME to improve commodity management at CAME warehouses. This will include creating an interface between CAME's current software SAGE SAARI and Medistock to allow data export and import between the both software programs. This will improve data analysis and allow more timely decision making
- Provide assistance to strengthen CAME and NMCP's capacity to forecast antimalarial drug and RDT needs and gaps
- Provide assistance to strengthen quality control, storage, distribution, and inventory management down to the health facility level

- Improve feedback and reporting on consumption/stocks from health facility to district and higher levels through strengthened supervision down to the health facility level

2. Build capacity of NMCP to monitor and supervise the redesigned logistics management information system: Provide technical and financial support to build the capacity of the NMCP to institutionalize LMIS monitoring and supervision. ($153,700);

3. Quarterly/monthly pre-positioning of malaria commodities: This support to CAME and NMCP will consist of implementing the "maximum-minimum inventory control systems", "delivery truck" or "informed push" distribution model (IPM), known in local communities as "pousse-pousse", and variation of "forced ordering inventory system" between mainly the health zonal depot (DRZ : *Depôt Répartiteur de Zone*) and health facilities and on the other hand, between CAME regional warehouses and health zonal depots (DRZ) which have limited accessibility. Consequently this is a barrier to maintaining adequate stock levels that are required by the LMIS. Implementng IPM can bring the supply source (a delivery truck loaded with supplies) closer to the place of demand (clients in health facilities) and can also streamline the steps between supply and demand. With a professional logistician of CAME managing stock and deliveries, health facilities no longer need to place orders and spend time picking up products. Key features of the IPM include the following:

- Dedicated logisticians from CAME restock facilities on a monthly basis to maintain a minimum level of one month of stock that is defined by the LMIS, around two months of maximum estimated supply needs
- Facilities only pay for the quantity of products that were sold, and keep the remaining funds
- Logisticians coach health facility workers, if needed, collect data on product consumption at the time of delivery, and report the data within 72 hours

Rather than submitting orders to the supplying facility, a resupply truck would visit health facilities at regular intervals (monthly/quarterly). During this visit, data would be collected, and stocks resupplied as needed. It is likely that $100,000 may not be enough to support the pre-positioning of commodities. However, this activity is not intended to be implemented nationally but targeted to health facilities with low rates of report completion or low quality reports according to the LMIS, EUV surveys or site supervision reports. This strategy will also be valuable for health zones which often do not have good accessibility by road or which are far from the CAME regional depot. To sustain this activity, CAME in collaboration with NMCP, will provide a strategic plan to continue this activity after CY 2015. This strategic plan should be developed by the end of the FY 2013. ($100,000)

4. Drug quality control testing: Provide support to National Laboratory for Quality Control to conduct routine testing of ACTs entering the port and spot-checks at facility levels. ($50,000).

C. MONITORING & EVALUATION/OPERATIONS RESEARCH

Background:

Benin's national malaria M&E strategic plan (*Plan de Suivi-Evaluation du Programme de la Lutte Contre le Paludisme 2011–2015*), includes a multi-institutional M&E Technical Working Group, epidemiologic surveillance, and monitoring of programmatic process indicators with routinely collected data and periodic evaluations of outcome indicators. Benin has three main sources of malaria information, all of which are supported and strengthened by PMI: (1) household and health facility surveys; (2) malaria surveillance from sentinel sites; and (3) the National HMIS. PMI support for entomological surveillance is described in the IRS section.

1) *Household and health facility surveys:* National household and health facility surveys provide the most reliable data. Standard household surveys most relevant to PMI include the DHSs, which were completed in 2006 (PMI's baseline survey) and 2012. These DHSs were methodologically similar except: (1) the 2006 survey was done at the end of the rainy season while the 2012 survey was done during the dry season; and (2) only the 2012 survey measured parasitemia prevalence. Future plans include a Malaria Indicator Survey (MIS) in 2014 and a DHS in 2016. Notably, UNICEF is planning to start a Multiple- Indicator Cluster Survey (MICS) in December 2013. If this MICS satisfies PMI's need for a survey between the 2012 and 2016 DHS's, then the 2014 MIS might be cancelled.

Another nationally-representative household survey (the Leadership and Development, or LEADD survey), based on the MIS methodology, was conducted in November 2010. However, methodological concerns, and the use of non-standard indicators may have compromised the validity of the results. The current PMI resident advisors are re-assessing the data from this survey, as they are a potentially important source of information.

Health facility surveys are conducted periodically. In 2009, a nationally-representative survey was done to assess the availability of malaria-related commodities, diagnostic capacity, and quality of malaria case management. Based on methodology similar to that used in the 2009 survey, a nationally-representative health facility survey is planned for the third quarter of 2013. In 2010 and 2011, EUV surveys of commodity availability were completed on small convenience samples of health facilities. A larger health facility survey on a nationally-representative sample of 128 health facilities was completed in April 2012.

2) *Sentinel surveillance:* In 2001, the WHO initiated malaria sentinel surveillance in six health zones, consisting of a large number of health facilities. By 2008, since the system was no longer functional, PMI and the World Bank Booster Program revived surveillance activities to provide data on more focused malaria indicators. Since January 2009, PMI funds the *Institut Régional de Santé Publique* (IRSP) in Benin to strengthen hospitals in five sentinel sites, enabling them to collect data on malaria morbidity and mortality.

A PMI internal evaluation conducted on data generated by the sites from September 2009 – June 2011 questioned the quality of the data. Specifically, a relatively low proportion of patients (63% in 2010 and 60% in 2011) with suspected malaria were tested, due in part to hospital stockouts of RDTs. The evaluation recommended that the NMCP revise the national policy to incorporate the new universal testing policy of all suspect cases regardless of the patient's age and the season (which have already been implemented) and ensure no RDT stockouts (which remains a consistent issue). Additionally IRSP should enforce focal points and non-focal points to test all patients meeting the case definition for suspected malaria. Lastly, sentinel site hospital directors/administration should reinforce universal testing for suspect cases and ensure no ACT and RDT stockouts. Beginning November 2011, administrative issues resulted in a lapse in the contract renewal for one year. During this time, data were collected but there was no sentinel site supervision, quality control, or auditing until after the contract was renewed in December 2012.

The sentinel sites are currently collecting and submitting data. Surveillance data during the period when a contract was not in place was systematically extracted from hospital registers and patient files, and complete supervision with quality control resumed in January 2013. During the period without data reporting, a rapid assessment of retrospective data at two sites showed that data collection (before October 2011) was timely, validated, updated correctly from laboratory diagnostic results, and was consistent with the pediatric, maternity, and medicine registries. However, it also revealed facility stockouts of commodities needed for surveillance, including RDTs, certain presentations of ACTs, SP and sometimes data collection forms. These rapid assessments also suggested that there may be challenges with the compliance of staff with NMCP treatment guidelines. Some health professionals may not be fully aware of the validity of RDTs, and microscopy may still be considered an important means of income for the hospital.

Given the uncertainty of the current system's ability to provide key surveillance data for a sustained period, a formal evaluation of the programmatic utility and the epidemiologic impact of this surveillance system on the prevention and control of malaria in Benin, is needed. A full evaluation of the sentinel sites, similar to the one that was conducted in 2011, will be carried out by the PMI M&E team during the next 12 months. The team will also provide recommendations on the continued support of the present surveillance system. The evaluation will determine whether progress has been made in addressing the 2011 recommendations and whether the current design is still practical for providing the desired data for trend analysis and informing programmatic decisions.

As the NMCP considers the sentinel sites a very valuable, important, and pertinent source of epidemiologic data, the NMCP has voiced its own desire to address these same issues. There are currently biweekly meetings with NMCP, ARM3 and the PMI/Benin M&E staff to examine the utility and impact of the current surveillance system and discuss what types of systematic or structural changes might be worthy of consideration.

3) *The National Health Management Information System (HMIS)*: The HMIS reports the number of malaria cases, deaths, and case fatality rates at the health facility level. Prior to PMI, the HMIS did not distinguish clinically diagnosed cases from those confirmed by laboratory testing. In addition, concerns existed about the accuracy, timeliness, and coverage of the data, as well as how the data were used for decision-making. With the support of PMI, the World Bank, and WHO, the NMCP is strengthening the malaria module of the national HMIS (i.e., the Routine Malaria Information System, or RMIS) to achieve the evaluation indicator goal of "at least 80% of public and private health facilities continuously and accurately report malaria data." Over the past two years, quality of data has improved significantly and the number of health facilities reporting exceeds the desired goal (details below). The system collects and reports on twenty key malaria indicators each month. The module was recently updated to include reports from community health workers; however reporting quality and completeness remains a challenge from this level. With support from PMI, quarterly RMIS newsletters are prepared to keep stakeholders abreast of the current malaria epidemiological situation in Benin.

4) *Other M&E Activities:* Additional M&E activities have been initiated to track progress in malaria control at the national and sub-national level. As previously mentioned, UNICEF is planning a MICS in 2013. This national household survey collects data for monitoring the situation of children and women, and includes malaria indicators similar to those collected through the DHS.

The USAID-funded community case management project introduced SMS messaging to track referrals made by CHWs in two health zones. During the initial pilot, approximately 100 CHWs were trained in the use of RDTs, 51 severe malaria referrals and 60 stock request alerts were received.

5) *Operations Research (OR):* PMI has supported the following OR studies:
- CREC is currently conducting an evaluation on the longevity of ITNs;
- A 2008 study to compare the effectiveness of ITNs and IRS (using bendiocarb) to ITN and insecticide-treated plastic sheets, full coverage with ITNs and usual coverage as per NMCP policy. Published results showed that households with ITNs and IRS or IRS and insecticide-treated plastic sheets had lower entomological inoculation rates compared to the full coverage with ITNs and usual coverage;[16] and
- A 2008 study to evaluate chemical (colorimetric) methodology for assessment of ITN bio-activity (verification that ITNs meet WHO standards for effective ITNs).[17]

Progress during the last 12 months:

M&E Support

Staff from PMI and NMCP worked closely on M&E issues, and PMI resident advisors were active participants in the M&E Technical Working Group. Due to administrative issues that caused a lapse in supervision and quality control audits of the five sentinel surveillance sites, the PMI resident advisors worked closely with the IRSP to re-establish supervisory support to the sites. As a result of the collaboration, a detailed strategy, work plan, and timeline were followed to improve data quality and reporting.

Survey Support

PMI provided financial support for a health facility survey to gauge commodity availability within health facilities. Results from this larger survey conducted in 2012 showed consistent stockouts of malaria commodities including RDTs, ACTs and SP. As a result, diagnoses of malaria usually did not follow the national treatment guidelines, which require testing using RDTs when malaria is suspected.

HMIS Support

During the previous 12 months, PMI provided technical and financial support to the RMIS. A desktop computer was installed at the NMCP and serves as the central storage

---

[16] Am. J. Trop. Med. Hyg 83(2), 2010, pp. 266-270
[17] Guidelines for evaluating deltamethrin levels on the surface of long-lasting insecticidal nets (LLINs) using the CDC colorimetric field assay. Available from entomology branch, Division of Parasitic Diseases and Malaria, CDC.

location for an integrated malaria data management system, which includes RMIS. From September 2012 to March 2013, the percentage of health facilities submitting a complete report increased from 64% to 85%. Quarterly data quality audits were conducted, and four quarterly RMIS bulletins were published. Additional training workshops for statisticians and data managers from each of the six departmental directorates were conducted to improve the use of data for making appropriate programmatic decisions.

Table F: Current and projected monitoring and evaluation data sources, 2008 – 2016

Data Source		Year[1]								
		2008	2009	2010	2011	2012	2013	2014	2015	2016
Household Surveys										
	LEADD			X (Report available)						
	Demographic and Health Survey (DHS)					X				X
	Multiple Indicator Cluster Survey (MICS)						X (non-PMI funded)			
	Malaria Indicator Survey (MIS)							X		
Other Surveys										
	End-Use Verification Survey (EUVS)			X (Report available)	X (Report available)		X	X		
	Health Facility Survey (HFS)		X (Report available)			X (Report available)	X			
	Impact Evaluation							X		

54

Data Source (cont'd)	Year[1]								
	2008	2009	2010	2011	2012	2013	2014	2015	2016
Malaria Surveillance and routine system support									
Health Information Management System (HMIS)	X	X	X	X	X (RMIS bulletins available)	X (RMIS bulletins available)	X	X	X
Sentinel Surveillance	X	X	X	X	----[2]	X	X		
Vector Resistance Surveillance	X	X	X	X	X	X	X		
Entomology Monitoring and Evaluation	X	X	X	X	X	X	X		
Logistics Management Information System (LMIS)					X	X	X	X	X
Other Data Sources									
Pilot Inpatient Health Facility Survey			X						
Routine Net Longevity Monitoring			X						
USAID Family Health Household Survey			X (non-PMI funded)	X (non-PMI funded)	X (non-PMI funded)				

Data Source (cont'd)	Year[1]								
	2008	2009	2010	2011	2012	2013	2014	2015	2016
Other Data Sources (cont'd)									
Africare Case Management Projects Household Survey		X (non – PMI funded)	X (non – PMI funded)	X (non – PMI funded)	X (non – PMI funded)				
LQAS Survey	X								
Integrated Modular Survey on Household Living Conditions		X			X				
Integrated Family Health Project (PISAF)		X	X	X	X				
UNICEF Accelerated Child Survival and Development Program			X	X	X				
Health Systems 20/20 Assessment					X				
BASICS midterm survey				X					

[1] Years listed reflects when PMI began in the country.
[2] Sentinel surveillance data was collected in 2012, however adminstrative challenges delayed the reporting of 2012 data until 2013.

Proposed activities with FY 2014 funding: ($462,100)

1. *Continue to strengthen health management information system:* PMI will continue to support the strengthening of of the overall HMIS. The funding will support the NMCP's efforts to implement PMI's recommendations, in particular: (1) providing training in database management, analysis and survey methodologies to enhance data accuracy and quality; (2) increased technical assistance and material support to the zonal offices; (3) creation of a final, detailed (and updated) indicator list with better case definitions; and (4) the creation and printing of written documentation (i.e., standard operating procedures, protocols) with specific tasks, dates, and person responsible for all levels participating in the RMIS. (*$200,000*);

2. *Support sentinel sites surveillance:* Five existing sentinel sites may continue to receive technical assistance to improve the capacity of these sites to collect reliable data on inpatient and outpatient malaria cases and deaths. Given the importance of increasing the malaria testing rate in Benin, including at sentinel sites, PMI is closely supervising the implementing partner agreement for effective scale up of malaria diagnosis. Due to unanticipated circumstances, this activity lapsed in 2012, and will be assessed in 2013 or early 2014 to evaluate its usefulness. The administrative issues resulted in the availability of funds for an additional year, however within the next 12 months, PMI will decide if the data quality and utility merits continued support in FY 2014. (*$100,000*);

3. *Conduct end-use verification surveys:* Quarterly monitoring of the availability and utilization of key antimalarial commodities at the health facility level. (*$150,000*); and

4. *Provide technical assistance for M&E:* CDC will conduct one technical assistance visit to support the NMCP with M&E. The PMI resident advisors, in collaboration with the NMCP, will determine technical priorities in M&E and will request an appropriate headquarters-based technical advisor. (*$12,100*).

D. BEHAVIOR CHANGE COMMUNICATION

Background:
In 2006, the NMCP developed a National Malaria BCC strategy as part of the National Malaria Control Plan and Strategy (2006-2011). This document was designed to be an integrated communication plan that would standardize messages and tools for all partners working on malaria in Benin. The NMCP is planning to develop and implement a new

integrated communication plan that accompanies the new National Malaria Control Plan and Strategy (2011-2015). The new integrated communication plan will include strategies for advocacy, BCC, and social mobilization. The NMCP would like to identify key behaviors and interventions that will be the basis of the integrated communication plan.

As part of the National Malaria Control Plan and Strategy, the NMCP has identified the following target indicators for BCC:
- 100% of heads of households in urban and rural areas know that ITNs are an effective means of prevention against malaria
- 100% of mothers and/or caregivers of children know the treatment for uncomplicated malaria
- 100% of mothers and/or caregivers of children know that treatment with ACTs requires positive confirmation with RDTs
- 100% of mothers and/or caregivers know the signs of malaria
- 100% of pregnant women in urban and rural areas are aware of IPTp and its advantages

Progress during the last 12 months:
Several studies have been conducted in Benin on the utilization of ANC services (attendance, regularity and adherence to taking medications) (by Africare in 2011, WHO in 2012 and ARM3 in 2013). The results of these studies generally show that non-compliance with IPTp using SP is due to sociocultural barriers and to barriers within the health system.

In collaboration with PMI partners, a literature review was conducted in 2012 by ARM3 to identify barriers to the use of IPTp and ITNs. The literature review identified barriers to the use of SP including, low use of prenatal care or non-compliance with ANC schedule, late consultation of pregnant women (the first consultation takes place after 32 weeks for 5% of women), abortion and premature birth ocurring before taking the second dose, stockouts of SP in health facilities, and ignorance of the public about the benefits of SP.

In order to gather accurate information on the attitudes and practices of pregnant women, ARM3 conducted a qualitative study to identify barriers to adherence to IPTp with SP in health zones in Atlantic and Littoral health zones of Cotonou I-IV, Toffo-Zè Allada and Ouidah-Kpomassè-Tori-Bossito. The study identified sociocultural and health system barriers, including:

Sociocultural barriers

- Lack of financial resources
- Ignorance of the benefits of EIC
- Late for the first ANC
- Non-compliance with appointments EIC and medical prescriptions

- Serological state of the pregnant woman
- Attendance at private health centers
- Population movements
- Rumors

Health system barriers

- Not free of MS
- Stockouts of SP
- Failure to recall ANC appointments for women
- High cost of consulting fees
- Side effects of SP
- Lack of hygiene in ANC service places
- Delay of some staff in their jobs
- Poor reception and treatment of pregnant women at ANC

The findings from this review were used to develop ARM3's BCC's strategy which includes the following objectives:

1. Support BCC interventions by the NMCP through: effective coordination of activities by the BCC Working Group; participation in activities by other existing working groups; harmonization of BCC/IEC messages, materials, and tools developed in Benin;
2. Increase community engagement in/mobilization for malaria prevention and treatment;
3. Increase the supply and use of ITNs through social marketing with private sector partners;
4. Upgrade BCC skills of health workers from private and public sectors at national and community levels, and provide supervision in the use of BCC guidelines;
5. Advocate for increased support for malaria control, by government authorities and key partners (reflected in support for coordination, availability of funds, allocation of human resources and development of public policies that support malaria mortality and morbidity reduction);
6. Develop and disseminate materials supporting BCC and Community Mobilization;
7. Monitor and evaluate the BCC and Community Mobilization Strategy.

In 2012, PMI provided support to revitalize the Communications TWG. The group is responsible for reviewing the technical content of all BCC messages pertaining to malaria and will play a key role in developing an updated integrated communication plan. Members of the group include the NMCP, PMI, Abt Associates, MCDI, Africare, Catholic Relief Services (CRS), Population Services International (PSI), the World Bank, WHO, UNICEF, and the Peace Corps. The TWG conducted a review of existing communication tools and materials as a first step toward updating all malaria communication tools and information. In addition, the TWG is working with the NMCP to complete the development of the new integrated communication plan that accompanies the National Malaria Control Plan and Strategy (2011-2015).

In implementing the objectives of the BCC strategy, PMI is supporting a multi-pronged approach to reach the maximum number of beneficiaries. BCC communication channels include mass media, banners, messaging through community health workers, interpersonal communication in health centers, community events, the involvement of opinion leaders, and social marketing. To this effect there has been a launch of several BCC activities. At the national level, a media campaign using TV spots and educational music videos on malaria have been launched. In addition, two radio programs, a radio magazine and a reality radio talk show, have been aired on national radio. To ensure appropriate, accurate and consistent message content for the radio programs, guides were provided to the radio stations. In addition, health providers from Atlantique and Littoral health departments participated in the programs as guest experts to provide answers to any questions that came up during the radio programs. PMI supported technical assistance in the production of all radio programs, including monitoring and supervision of recording, editing, and airing.

In addition, PMI provided support in the development and production of flyers on SP for IPTp, ITNs and ACTs. The flyers are being made available to health centers with the goal of being distributed to clients that come for consultations. To date, 33,100 ITN, 40,000 SP and 33,100 ACT flyers have been distributed. In addition to flyers, banners have been produced for use at community events. The PMI also supported community social mobilization events, including a caravan for social mobilization, as well as community theatre events. In addition, selected NGOs have been engaged to conduct community dialogue to promote key malaria-related practices and behaviors among community members.

For communication activities related to IRS, PMI adopted a new and streamlined approach under which the majority of IRS agents trained as spray operators are also used for community mobilization, structure identification, and enumeration activities, which has improved the link between community mobilization and spray operations. The NMCP and ARM3 are planning to conduct an OMNIBUS survey, which is designed to gain insight and collect quantitative data on a wide variety of subjects during the same interview. This survey will be administered during the first trimester of project year three, to try and gauge the impact of BCC activities in selected areas. The survey will look at exposures to mass media, community mobilization and interpersonal communication activities on several target behaviors. The findings will be used to guide planning and review of communication interventions.

Challenges, opportunities, and threats:
Preliminary results from the most recent DHS shows an improvement of behaviors around the use of ITNs, with the percentage of those who slept under an ITN the night before the survey increasing in both children under five years of age (from 20% to 70%) and in pregnant women (from 20% to 75%). Unfortunately, with treatment of children under five with fever, only 7% received antimalarial drugs the same or the next day. This contrast in data illustrates both an opportunity and challenge for BCC to reinforce desired behaviors around the proper and consistent use of malaria products and services. The development and rollout of the new communication strategy will provide an opportunity for partners and stakeholders to review current barriers around these and other malaria interventions and will also provide an opportunity to develop interventions that address specific barriers.

Plans and justification:
With FY 2014 funding, PMI will support the roll-out of the new national integrated communication strategy. As part of these efforts, PMI will support the continued roll-out of the new integrated communication plan, through ARM3. ARM3 will provide technical assistance through the provision of reference documents and through technical assistance in developing BCC strategies. In addition ARM3 will facilitate partner meetings to discuss the development of the strategy as well as providing continuous input/feedback until completion of the strategy, as well as continuous M&E of all BCC-supported activities. The PMI team will receive input and support from PMI/Washington as the partners in country move forward with collecting BCC data and providing feedback to specific programs.

In line with the National Malaria Control Plan and Strategy, activities will be focused on raising awareness of households on the importance of the use of ITNs, recognizing signs of malaria, increasing care-seeking behavior within 24 hours of the onset of fever, and improving IPTp coverage by encouraging mothers to attend ANC early. PMI will also continue its support for community mobilization for IRS. Overall, PMI-supported BCC activities will be implemented at both the national and community levels.

Proposed activities with FY 2014 funding: ($530,000)

1. *Support household visits and group education to promote net use and malaria prevention; recognizing signs of malaria; increasing care-seeking behavior; and encouraging ANC attendance and IPTp through women's groups, CHWs, and mass media:* To promote the hang-up, use, and maintenance of ITNs, PMI will continue to

employ a multipronged approach to behavior change. BCC strategies will be focused at the community level, but will use mass media approaches when appropriate. Messages will focus on explaining correct care and use of nets and emphasizing the importance of ITN use among children under five and pregnant women, as well as all other members of a household. In urban areas, PMI will contract with local NGOs with experience in BCC to conduct net promotion activities. In areas where CHWs are being trained to treat malaria, PMI will utilize these community agents to conduct household visits and follow-up activities. In addition to interpersonal communication for year-round net use, PMI will also target pregnant mothers to attend ANC early to receive IPTp and work with caregivers to ensure that febrile children are brought in for treatment within 24 hours of the onset of fever. This activity will include support for community-level approaches, such as training of community-based workers and mass media campaigns over public radio. Immunization outreach sessions will be used as opportunities for educating women. ($200,000);

2. *Support the roll-out of the national malaria communication strategy.* To raise national awareness about the importance of IPTp, early care-seeking, necessity of confirmatory testing, completion of treatment, and use of mosquito nets through national television and radio programs and national malaria events such as Africa Malaria Day ($300,000); and

3. *Support Peace Corps BCC activities.* Following the success of the 2012 collaboration with NMCP for the universal distribution of ITNs, Peace Corps (PC) Benin Against Malaria program will fully engage in Peace Corps Africa Region's Stomp Out Malaria initiative, with the goal of having all 115 Peace Corps volunteers (PCVs) implementing at least one evidence-based community-level malaria activity per year to sustainably address malaria in Benin and improve the health status of Beninese families. All PCVs receive training and support to conduct malaria activities related to their own project framework. Formative community assessments have revealed gaps in distribution and use of ITNs. All PCVs will conduct similar assessments to identify gaps in coverage and ITN use in communities where PCVs are based. Brief surveys will be adminstered before implementing malaria activities in a community. PCVs will work with schools and school groups, health centers, community-based associations, care groups, and other community groups to design, implement, and evaluate malaria activities, and as always, will build capacity building and sustainability into their interventions. This widened target population has full approval from the NMCP. PC Benin Against Malaria aims to promote malaria prevention and early treatment activities in PCV communities in line with the NMCP policy. PC Benin Against Malaria intends to accomplish the following: (1) identify gaps in ITN coverage and use; (2) develop community-wide campaigns to encourage

ITN use, early and appropriate treatment, and other preventive messaging; and (3) implement effective ITN distributions in PCV communities as needed based on community assessment. ($30,000).

E. HEALTH SYSTEMS STRENGTHENING/CAPACITY BUILDING

Background:

PMI is a component program of Benin's GHI country strategy. Health systems strengthening (HSS), and women, girls, and gender equality are the two key principles chosen as emphases in the implementation of the GHI strategy. In the last three years, the NMCP and PMI have focused on three major challenges of the NMCP as a unit within Benin's health system: (1) the lack of adequate human resource capacity – both in numbers and skills sets – to plan, manage, and coordinate a comprehensive malaria program; (2) the collection, management and use of health information for M&E and surveillance purposes; and (3) the management of the health commodities supply chain, which is especially weak at the periphery, resulting in stockouts, and expiration of drugs and RDTs. With these priorities in mind, PMI has worked in close collaboration with the GOB and other stakeholders (WHO, the Global Fund, UNICEF, bilateral partners, and NGOs) to reduce these barriers to reinforce the delivery of malaria interventions. The PMI's support in strengthening the health system and the integration of malaria interventions with other programs has been proven to have positive spill-over effects to other MOH units and health programs, especially child and maternal health.

Many donors are working to strengthen Benin's public sector health system. One important mechanism is the Health Compact, signed in 2011, which was promoted by health-focused multilateral organizations and European donors to strengthen the health system. Important signatories include: the Global Fund, the Coopération Technique Belge, the World Bank, the Global Alliance for Vaccines and Immunizations, and more recently, the Coopération Francaise, through their recently approved Muskoka Initiative. The purpose of the compact is to maximize aid effectiveness to the health sector through the support of country systems. USAID/Benin is not a signatory to the compact and is still in the early stages of implementing procurement reforms under USAID Forward. The MOH is a principal recipient under Benin's Global Fund Round 9 grant that includes an HSS component. This will complement the Results-Based Financing arrangements already approved and ready to be implemented by the Global Alliance for Vaccines and Immunizations (two health zones) and the Coopération Technique Belge (five health zones). The World Bank is already implementing a $22.8 million grant project to increase the coverage of quality maternal and neonatal health services in eight health zones in Benin. Two health zones remain uncovered.

Universal health care financing through the *Régime d'Assurance Maladie Universelle* is a new MOH priority, and was launched by President Yayi Boni on December 19, 2011. It is based on the existing mutuelles, the grassroots health cooperatives supported by several aid organizations in Benin including USAID, Coopération Suisse, Coopération Technique Belge, and UNICEF. This initiative will have a great impact on the financing of malaria services throughout the country.

Progress during the last 12 months:
In response to the NMCP's (and MOH's) various human resource challenges, PMI invested in the training of several key NMCP staff. Key areas of interest were M&E, supply chain management system (for essential antimalarial drugs, bed nets, and diagnostic equipment), and program management. Some of the activities were the following: two workshops for 35 departmental level staff to receive training in leadership and management; a workshop on the use of NetCalc to forecast the number of ITNs; individual and group mentoring on logistical software being used; two key staff trained in Logistics and Management in Ouagadougou; the revival of the Technical Working Groups (TWGs): M&E, Supply Chain Management, Behavior Change and Communication, and Case Management; the resumption of PMI's commitment to increase staff presence at the NMCP through the CDC resident advisor; the participation of NMCP staff in PMI quarterly program reviews, the MOP planning exercise, the Integrated Annual Work Plan workshop and other malaria meetings. The TWGs now have scheduled meetings and the Supply Chain Management TWG is meeting weekly to monitor stocks. Also, PMI participated in the committee that revised the National Strategic Plan and helped recruit an Information Management consultant who is currently assisting the NMCP.

With regard to improving the health information system, PMI supported the NMCP in conducting an evaluation of the existing health information system. Some of the findings included: lack of a centralized database at the NMCP; different health information databases stored on the personal computers of staff; inconsistency in data collection for some databases; and a low level of motivation among staff responsible for collecting data. The results of this evaluation are being used to make improvements in the system, including developing scopes of work for positions to be filled; the re-establishment of internet connection at the NMCP; the provision of updated hardware; and continued training of personnel responsible for data collection and management.

Finally, as concerns management of the supply chain, PMI has supported the NMCP and CAME by reviewing current plans and assisting in development of better tracking tools. The results of these actions have helped the NMCP better identify current weaknesses and allowed them to propose actions to remedy them. The improved tracking tools are currently being evaluated to see if improvements in the supply chain are taking place. Also, upcoming EUVs should shed light on whether improvements in commodity distribution to peripheral levels are occurring.

Challenges, opportunities, and threats:
Benin has been fortunate to have several major technical and financial partners in recent years. However, the donor environment has changed. At this juncture, it is important to build on the leadership, management, and governance (LMG) capacities in country. The LMG project, which will be formally launched in July 2013, will focus on developing the leadership and management capacity of MOH staff. Through mentoring and coaching by seasoned health program managers embedded within the MOH, the values, attitudes and skills of leaders will improve governance and service delivery results. NMCP program managers will join their peers in the Directorates for Mother and Child Health, Plan and Prospective, and National Vaccination and Primary Health Care as targets for this project. This will be the foundation for sustainable leadership to maintain the gains achieved in controlling malaria in Benin.

Plans and justification:
In the next year, PMI will focus on improving capacity within the MOH in the areas of leadership, management, and governance. In addition, PMI will work with the MOH to identify key staff, as well as collaborate with the NMCP, to improve leadership across NMCP functions: information systems, supply chain management, communications, case management, and program development. These are the elements that are needed to ensure that malaria treatment and prevention activities are being sustainably scaled up. This LMG support will be provided through a multi-donor consortium ensuring a broad-based and long-term commitment that will accompany these objectives to completion. The PMI will also support the training of department- and health zone-level staff responsible for malaria services in basic epidemiology, program management, and monitoring. The combined effect of these HSS activities is to enable the NMCP to shape, own, manage, and monitor malaria services at the central, district, and health center levels.

Proposed activities with FY 2014 funding: ($200,000)

1. *Support capacity building of the NMCP:* PMI will continue to provide support for the staff training plan that was developed by the NMCP. The focus will include LMG training in logistics, information systems, and support for the TWGs. Also, PMI will provide support for attendance at conferences and workshops related to logistics management. ($200,000).

F. STAFFING AND ADMINISTRATION

Two health professionals serve as resident advisors to oversee the PMI team in Benin, one representing CDC and one representing USAID. In addition, one FSN works as part of the PMI team. All PMI staff members are part of a single inter-agency team led by the USAID Mission Director or his/her designee in country. The PMI team shares responsibility for development and implementation of PMI strategies and work plans, coordination with national authorities, managing collaborating agencies and supervising day-to-day activities. Candidates for the resident advisor positions (whether initial hires or replacements) are evaluated and/or interviewed jointly by USAID and CDC and both agencies are involved in hiring decisions, with the final decision made by the individual agency.

PMI professional staff work together to oversee all technical and administrative aspects of PMI, including finalizing details of project design, implementing malaria prevention and treatment activities, monitoring and evaluation of outcomes and impact, reporting of results, and providing guidance to PMI partners.

The PMI lead in Benin is the USAID Mission Director. The two PMI resident advisors, one from USAID and one from CDC, report to the Senior USAID Health Officer for day-to-day leadership, and work together as a part of a single interagency team. The technical expertise housed in Atlanta and Washington guides PMI programmatic efforts and thus overall technical guidance for both resident advisors falls to the PMI staff in Atlanta and Washington. Since CDC resident advisors are CDC employees (CDC USDD—38), responsibility for completing official performance reviews lies with the CDC West Africa Regional Coordinator in Atlanta. He/She is expected to rely upon input from PMI staff across the two agencies that work closely day in and day out with the CDC resident advisor and thus best positioned to comment on the Advisor's performance.

The two PMI resident advisors are based within the USAID health office and are expected to spend approximately half their time sitting with and providing technical assistance to the national malaria control programs and partners.

Locally-hired staff to support PMI activities either in Ministries or in USAID will be approved by the USAID Mission Director. Because of the need to adhere to specific country policies and USAID accounting regulations, any transfer of PMI funds directly to Ministries or host governments will need to be approved by the USAID Mission Director and Controller, in addition to the PMI Coordinator.

Proposed activities with FY 2014 funding: ($1,222,000)

1. *USAID technical staff:* Support one resident advisor and malaria-specific staff member. ($500,000);

2. *CDC technical staff*: Support one resident advisor. ($400,000); and

3. *FSN staff and other in-country administrative expenses*: Cover ICASS costs. ($322,000).

G. Table 1
President's Malaria Initiative – *Benin*
FY 2014 Budget Breakdown by Partner ($16,100,000)

Partner Organization	Geographic Area	Activity	Budget
DELIVER	Nationwide	Procure ITNs, SP, RDTs, ACTs, microscopes, and reagents	$6,979,000
ARM3	Nationwide	Support training, supervision, BCC, supply chain management, diagnostics, iCCM, health systems strengthening, capacity building, and M&E	$2,400,000
IRS IQC	9 Communes in Atacora	Support IRS	$4,000,000
CREC	9 Communes in Atacora	Support vector surveillance and insecticide resistance monitoring	$120,000
USP	Nationwide	Support drug quality control	$50,000
Community PIHI Implementing Organizations	TBD	Support an iCCM program in five health zones, including BCC	$600,000
NMCP	National	Strengthen HMIS and LMIS supervision	$553,700
CAME	TBD	TBD	$100,000
CDC IAA	National	Technical assistance for entomology and M&E	$45,300
CDC IAA	National	Support for one resident advisor	$400,000
USAID	National	Support for one resident advisor and locally-hired staff and other administrative costs	$822,000
Peace Corps	TBD	BCC	$30,000

TOTAL	$16,100,000

G. Table 2

President's Malaria Initiative – *Benin*

Planned Obligations for FY 2014 ($16,100,000)

Proposed Activity	Mechanism	Budget	Geographic Area	Description of Activity
		PREVENTION		
Insecticide-Treated Nets				
1. Procurement ITNs	DELIVER Task Order #7	3,600,000	National	Procurement of 800,000 ITNs for delivery through routine services at health facilities. This includes delivery up to the health facility.
	Subtotal: ITNs	**$3,600,000**		
Indoor Residual Spraying				
1a. IRS implementation	IRS IQC	4,000,000	Nine communes in Atacora (northern Benin)	One round of IRS in northern Benin; includes training for personnel, equipment/insecticide procurement, community mobilization, and IRS implementation
1b. Support community mobilization for IRS	IRS IQC	(included in IRS implementation costs)	Nine communes in Atacora	Preparation and sensitization of communities being targeted for IRS to ensure compliance and high

Proposed Activity	Mechanism	Budget	Geographic Area	Description of Activity
			(northern Benin)	coverage
2. Entomological monitoring for spray areas and selected sentinel sites.	CREC	120,000	Nine communes in Atacora (northern Benin)	Entomological monitoring in the spray areas and sentinel sites. CREC will involve NMCP personnel trained in entomology
3. Technical assistance for vector control	CDC IAA	33,200	IRS Areas	Funding for two technical assistance visits to monitor IRS and entomological surveillance as well as purchase of supplies, equipment and reagents that are otherwise difficult to obtain in Benin
	Subtotal: IRS	**$4,153,200**		
Malaria in Pregnancy				
1. Procure SP	DELIVER	124,000	Nationwide	Procure approximately 1,050,000 doses of SP treatments to cover 2014 needs (# of pregnancies estimated at 525,000 in 2014). SP bought will also be available to the public and private sector according to the national policy
2. Provide support for supervision and refresher training of health workers in IPTp to improve quality of service	ARM3	Costs covered in Case Management-Treatment section	Nationwide	On-site supervision and refresher training of healthcare workers including benchmark assessments, on-the-spot training on new algorithm, and coaching
Subtotal: Malaria in Pregnancy		**$124,000**		

Proposed Activity	Mechanism	Budget	Geographic Area	Description of Activity
CASE MANAGEMENT				
Diagnosis				
1. Procure Rapid Diagnostic Tests (RDTs)	DELIVER	1,110,000	Nationwide	Procure 1.7 million RDTs to cover needs for 2015
2. Procure microscopes and laboratory reagents	DELIVER	45,000	Nationwide	Procure 15 microscope kits that include microscopes and reagents. Additional laboratory reagents will be provided for use with existing microscopes
3. Support supervision and strengthening of malaria diagnostic activities	ARM3	200,000	Nationwide	Supervision, development of policies, standard operating procedures, maintenance of microscopes, training, conduct periodic review of malaria diagnostics, and quality control of slides/RDTs
Subtotal: Diagnostics		**$1,355,000**		
Treatment				
1. Procure ACTs	DELIVER	2,100,000	Nationwide	Procurement of approximately 1.5 million ACT treatments

Proposed Activity	Mechanism	Budget	Geographic Area	Description of Activity
2. Support subsidization of free malaria treatment	ARM3	200,000	TBD	As part of the new national policy to provide "free" treatment to children under five and pregnant women, PMI will provide subsidies to selected facilities
3. Support quality improvement and supervision of healthcare workers at the facility level	ARM3	500,000	Nationwide	On-site supervision of healthcare workers including benchmark assessments, on-the-spot training on new algorithm, and coaching including supervision of diagnostics activities
4. Support malaria training for health workers	ARM3	150,000	Nationwide	Support training of health workers on new case management guidelines, which will target outpatient health facilities
5. Support integrated management of childhood illness training	ARM3	100,000	Nationwide	Support in-service training of health workers in integrated management of childhood illness
6. Support community case management of malaria, pneumonia and diarrhea	Community PIHI Implementing Organizations (TBD)	400,000	Selected HZs	Support an iCCM program in five health zones, which complements the Global Fund iCCM program for malaria
7. Support community case management of malaria, pneumonia and diarrhea	ARM3	150,000	Nationwide	Technical assistance to NGOs implementing an iCCM program in five health zones, which complements the Global Fund iCCM program for malaria

Proposed Activity	Mechanism	Budget	Geographic Area	Description of Activity
Subtotal: Treatment		**$3,600,000**		
Pharmaceutical Management				
1.Strengthen logistics management information system and supply chain management	ARM3	550,000	Nationwide	Strengthen the national logistics management information system as well as the supply chain management system from the central level down to the health facilities through the improvement of supply chain management, forecasting/quantifying, tracking, and storage of malaria commodities (ACTs, SP, RDTs)
2. LMIS Supervision	NMCP	153,700	Nationwide	
3. Prepositioning of commodities to the zonal level (health facilities and DRZ) or Informed Push Distribution Model (IPM)	CAME	100,000	TBD	Provide support to NMCP through CAME to improve consumption data quality and the health facilities completeness report rate by using a Push distribution system model for the health facilities revealed by the Malaria LMIS as the poor performers
4. Drug quality control testing	USP	50,000	Nationwide	Provide support to the national laboratory for quality control to conduct routine testing of ACTs entering the port and spot checks at facilities
Subtotal: Pharmaceutical Management		**$853,700**		

Proposed Activity	Mechanism	Budget	Geographic Area	Description of Activity
MONITORING AND EVALUATION/OPERATIONS RESEARCH				
1. Strengthen HMIS	NMCP	200,000	Nationwide	Strengthen procedures and indicators for malaria in the HMIS and comprehensive strengthening of system overall, including RMIS
2. Support sentinel sites surveillance	ARM3	100,000	Nationwide	Technical assistance to five sites for collection of reliable data on inpatient malaria cases and deaths. This support is conditional based upon 2013 performance
3. Conduct EUV surveys	ARM3	150,000	Nationwide	Monitoring of availability and utilization of key antimalarial commodities at the health facility level
4. Provide technical assistance for M&E	CDC IAA	12,100	Nationwide	Funding for one CDC advisor to provide technical assistance for M&E
Subtotal: M&E/OR		**$462,100**		
BEHAVIOUR CHANGE COMMUNICATION				
1. Support development and implementation of new integrated communication strategy.	Community PIHI Implementing Organizations	200,000	Nationwide	Support household visits and group education to promote net use and malaria prevention, recognizing signs of malaria and increasing care seeking behavior and encouraging ANC attendance and IPTp through women's groups, CHWs, and

Proposed Activity	Mechanism	Budget	Geographic Area	Description of Activity
				mass media
2. National level BCC TA	ARM3	300,000	Nationwide	Support mass media (including local radio spots), as well as community-level approaches, such as training of community-based workers to promote net use, to recognize signs of malaria, to increase care seeking behavior and to encourage ANC attendance and IPTp through women's groups, CHWs, and mass media
3. Peace Corps BCC	Peace Corps	30,000		
Subtotal: BCC		$530,000		
HEALTH SYSTEMS STRENGTHENING/CAPACITY BUILDING				
1. Support capacity building of NMCP including M&E System	NMCP	200,000		Continued support for training, including online training in logistics/management, conferences, workshops, equipment (i.e., computers), and human resource capacity building. M&E strengthening will include a database, data manager, and an M&E website
Subtotal: HSS/Capacity Building		$200,000		
STAFFING AND ADMINISTRATION				
1. USAID Technical Staff	USAID	500,000		Support for one USAID PMI Advisor and one USAID locally-hired senior malaria advisor as well
2. CDC Technical Staff	CDC IAA	400,000		as one CDC PMI Advisor, and all related local

Proposed Activity	Mechanism	Budget	Geographic Area	Description of Activity
3. FSN staff and other in-country administrative expenses	USAID	322,000		costs to sitting in USAID Mission.
Subtotal: Staffing and Administration		$1,222,000		
GRAND TOTAL		$16,100,000